Semi-Tropic Spiritualists

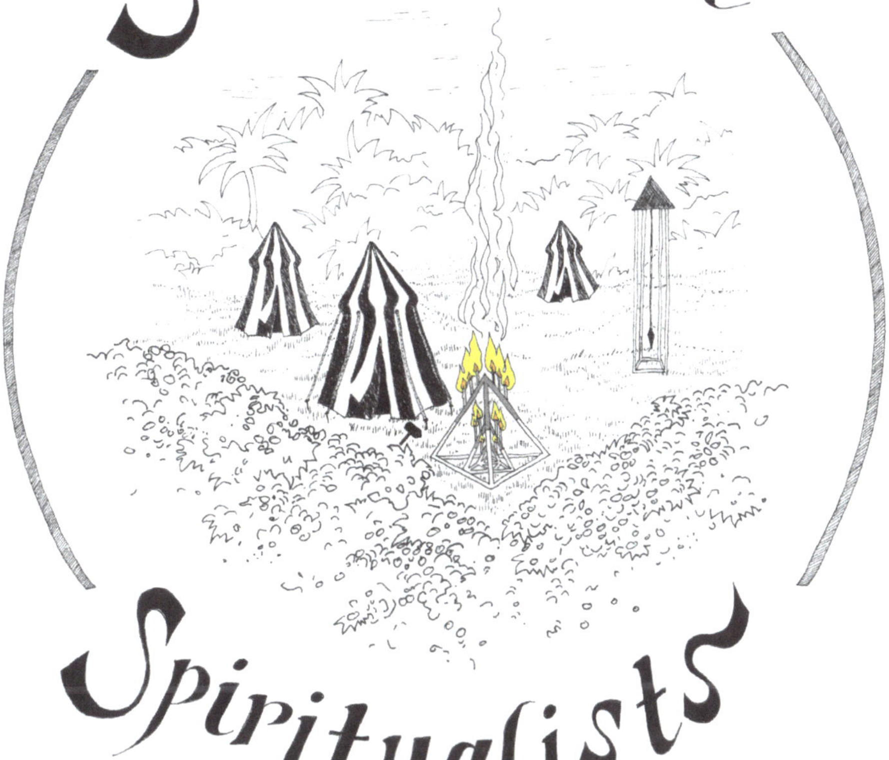

Astri Swendsrud & Quinn Gomez-Heitzeberg

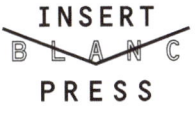

Los Angeles

Semi-Tropic Spirtualist Guidebook
© 2018 Astri Swendsrud and Quinn Gomez-Heitzeberg
Insert Blanc Press
ISBN: 978-1-947322-93-6

The Semi-Tropic Spiritualist Guide to Symbols and their Interpretation

Hammer
Labor
Foundation

Palm Tree
History
Legacy

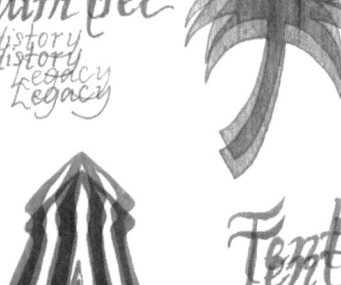

Tent
Camp
Community

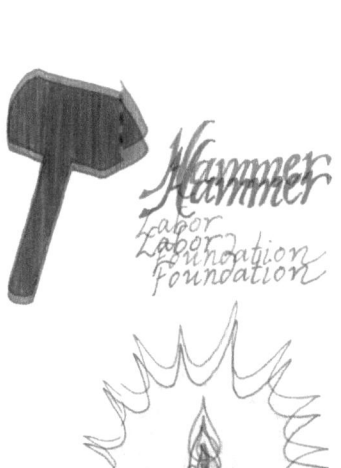
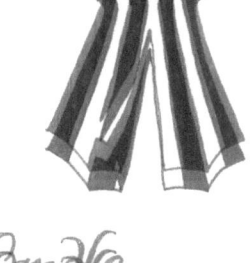

Candle
Knowledge
Learning

Pendulum
Mystery
Divination

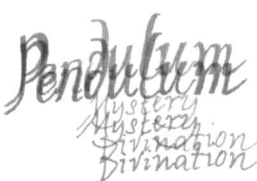

Triple Pyramid
Exploration
Ascension

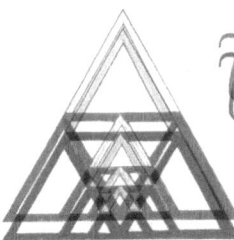

Semi-Tropic Spiritualists in California

Semi~Tropic Spiritualist Guidebook

Introduction: Semi-Tropic Park (exterior)	7
1. Los Angeles (past)	13
2. Los Angeles (present)	21
3. Desert (past)	33
4. Los Angeles (present)	47
5. The Hatchery	63
6. Irvine	75
7. Desert (present)	87
8. Los Angeles (future)	107
Conclusion: Semi-Tropic Park (interior)	117

Introduction: Semi-Tropic Park (exterior)

In 1905, the Semi-Tropic Spiritualist Association purchased a tract of land outside the city limits of Los Angeles. The tract was divided into small parcels for permanent dwellings, which surrounded a large central park. This park was set aside as a public meeting place for the Semi-Tropic Spiritualists to host camp meetings, including lectures, séances, investigations and tests. At this site, a community formed around a shared search for knowledge extending beyond the conscious mind.

In 2012, we saw an article online referencing the development of the "Semi-Tropic Spiritualist Tract," a previously unoccupied plot of land located in the Echo Park neighborhood of Los Angeles. As artists whose individual practices had addressed esoteric beliefs such as Spiritualism, this name caught our attention. Further research lead to blog posts by a local community activist documenting years of attempts to preserve the space, which had remained open land since the days of the original Semi-Tropic Spiritualists. However, by the time we discovered this site, the Artís townhouse complex was already in progress.

Though the last physical traces of the Semi-Tropic Spiritualists in Los Angeles were disappearing with their park, we decided to re-claim their name and their mission. We were interested in Spiritualism and its history as a model for exploring ideas of faith and skepticism, belief and charlatanism, as well as for the development of a space dedicated to investigation and the search for knowledge.

Because we discovered the Semi-Tropic Spiritualists through the loss of our home site, our project has always been nomadic. We create our own campsites and temporary communities, often traveling to other locations of alternative, visionary activities, such as the utopian ruins of Llano del Rio, and the complex, conflicted remnants of The Hatchery in Badger, CA. Our placelessness has allowed the project to grow and develop freely and expansively. However, we are always drawn back to sites of origin, to the physical traces left behind. The development of the Semi-Tropic Spiritualist Tract marks not only the disappearance of rare open land within the city, but also the loss of historical memory and intangible spiritual energy. In this guidebook, we follow the Semi-Tropic Spiritualist's journeys across California, creating test-sites to re-encounter history, examine the complexities that occur when metaphysical and utopian ideals manifest in physical spaces, and seek out places of alternative social possibility and new models for being in the world.

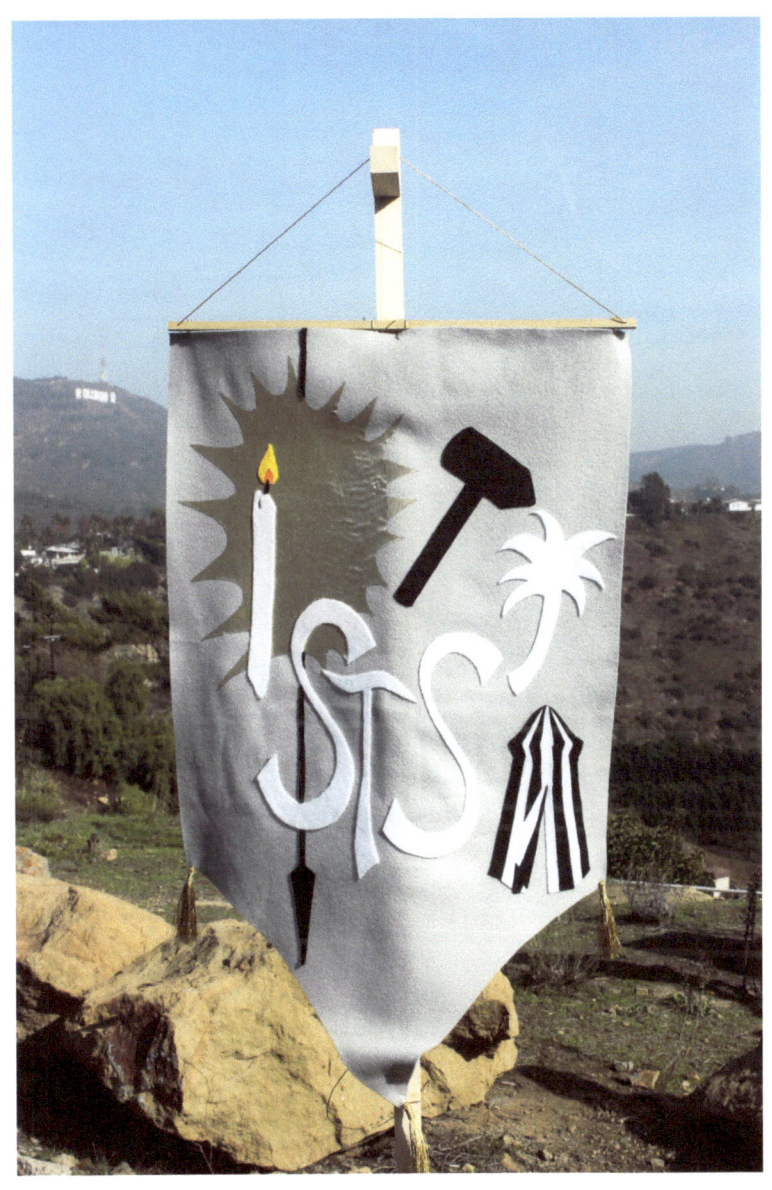

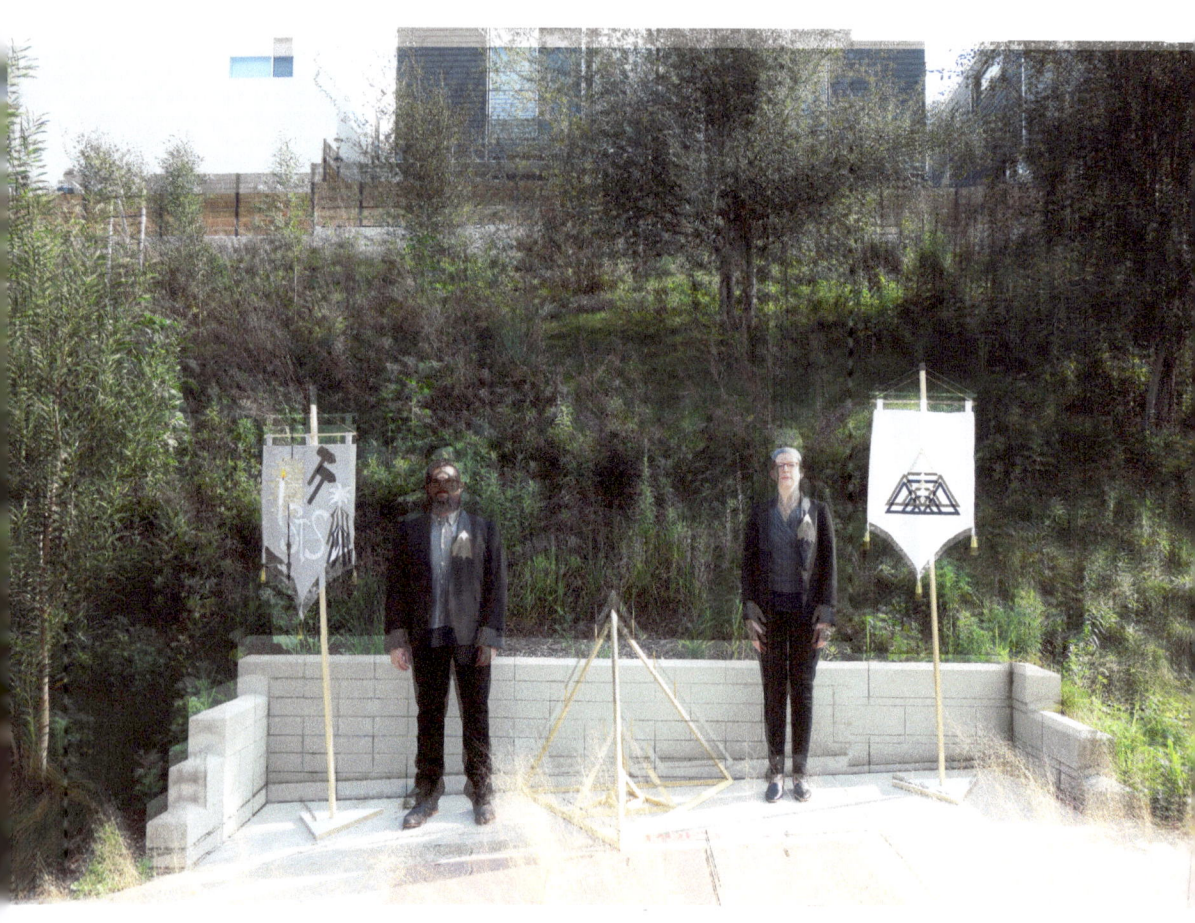

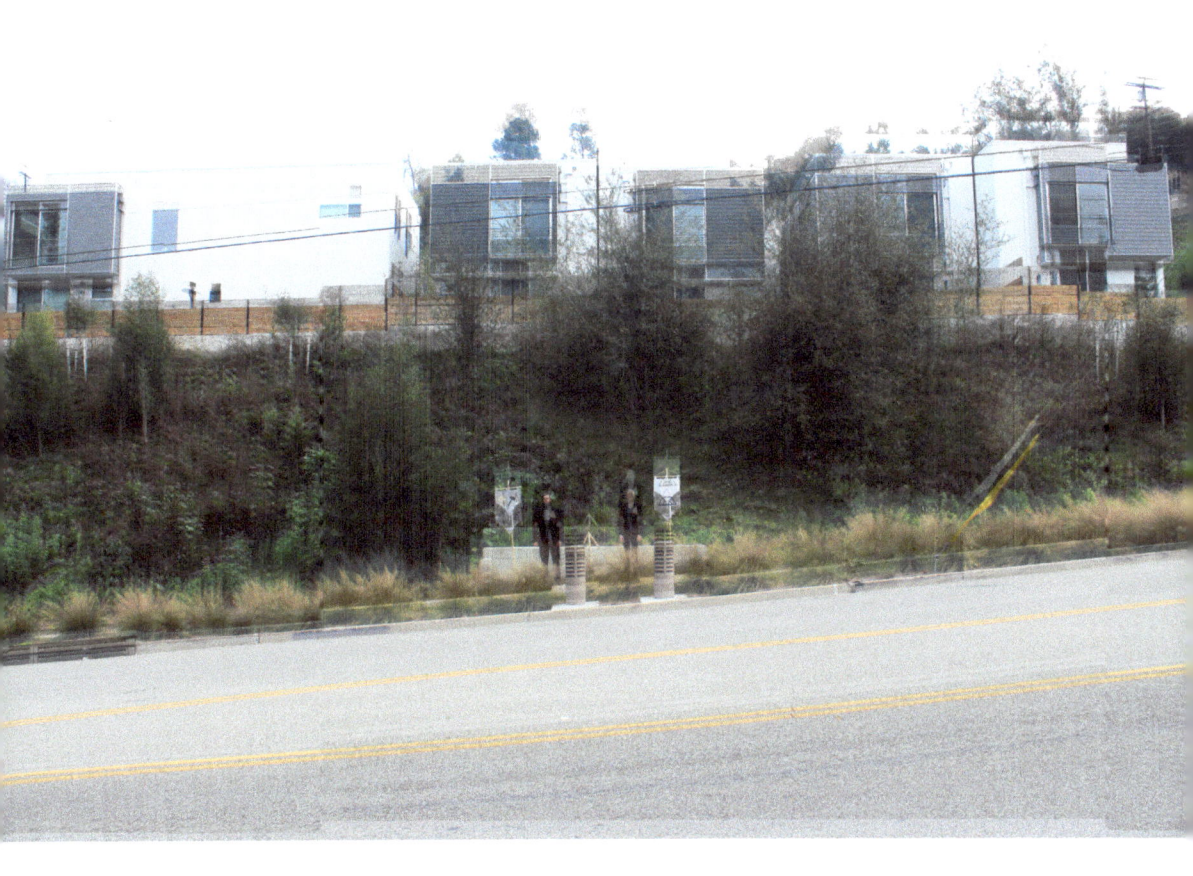

1.
Los Angeles
(past)

Semi-Tropic Spiritualist Test Site No. 1

Spiritualism, which referred to itself as a science, a philosophy and a religion, became popular in the United States during the 19th century. It began in upstate New York with the philosophy of Andrew Jackson Davis and the spirit communications of the Fox Sisters. Unlike traditional religions, which often position themselves as an authoritative voice of answers, Spiritualism presented an open process of discovery in which anyone could participate.

As the 20th century began and Spiritualism started to decline on the East Coast, many of its adherents traveled west to California to find a more open and progressive environment to practice and share their beliefs. The vast, open spaces of California allowed room for Spiritualist communities, like Harmony Grove, Summerland and Semi-Tropic Park, to develop as gathering points for the California Spiritualists to continue their search for new models of knowledge and new forms of communal living.

Following the example of the original Semi-Tropic Spiritualists, we created an encampment at the city's edge, looking back to the historic core of Los Angeles and the sites of early Spiritualist and metaphysical activity. The public was invited to interact with a series of divination tools available at our site, participating in a search for lost or hidden locations of spiritual energy and practice.

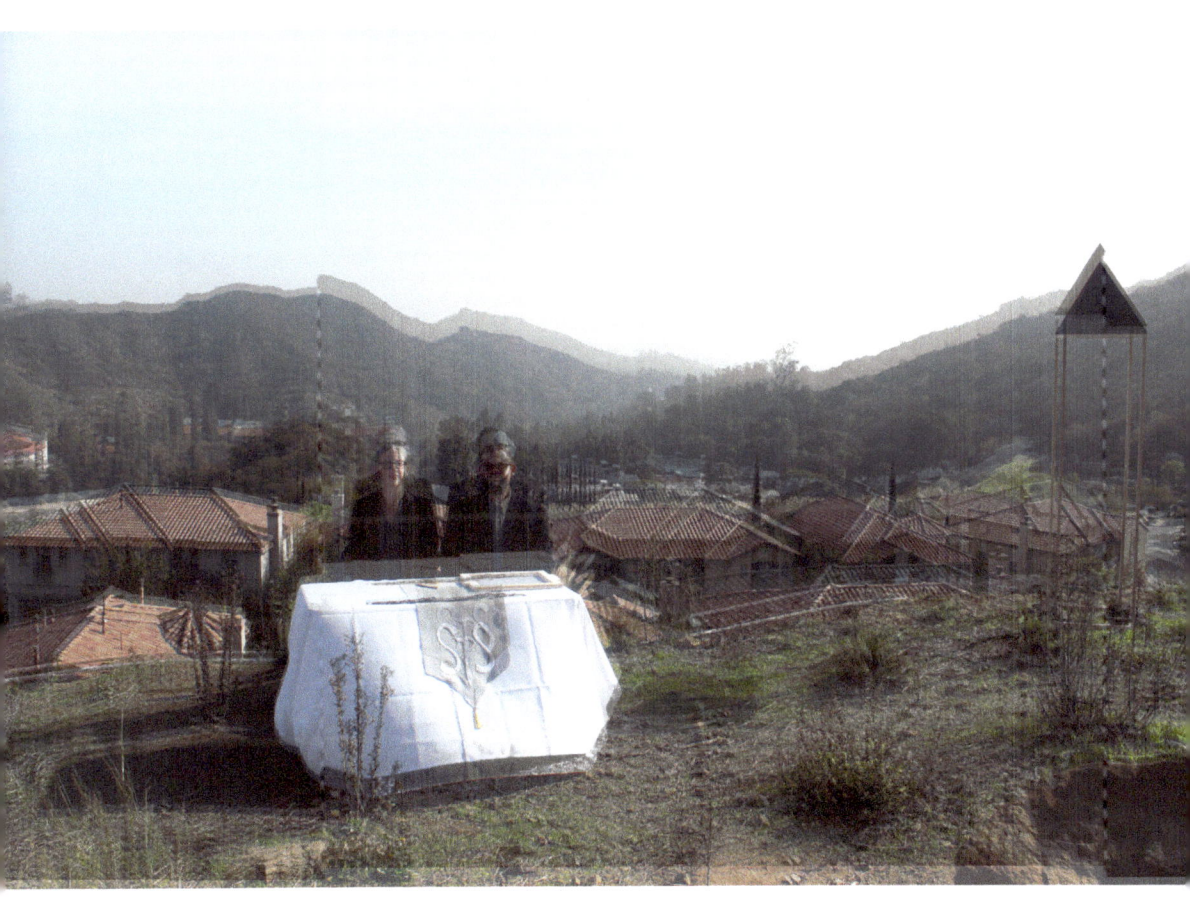

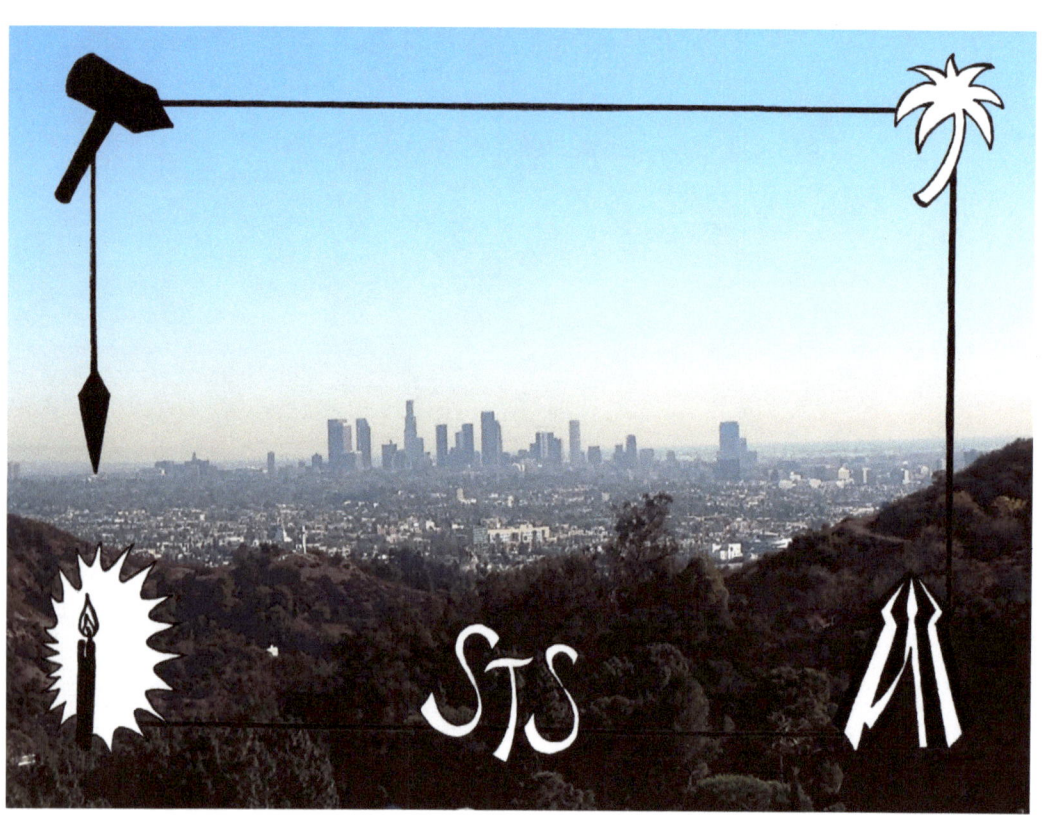

Semi-Tropic Spiritualist Test Site No. 1
A project by Astri Swendsrud and Quinn Gomez-Heitzeberg

1. Services at Semi-Tropic Park
    Take Edendale cars to end of line
2. The Spiritual Society of Truth-Seekers
    Mammoth Hall, 517 S. Broadway
3. Madame May Van Unken of the Van Unken Institute
    *stopping at the Hotel Lincoln, 207 S. Hill Street,
    for the development of Man's Higher Instincts*
4. Mrs. Belle Edwards, the marvelous platform test psychic
    Caledonia Hall, 119-1/2 S. Spring Street
5. Theosophical Society in America
    142 S. Broadway
6. Society Spiritual Progression
    Instruction in Practical Occultism, 584 S. Hill Street
7. People's Spiritualist Church
    Burbank Hall, 542 S. Main Street
8. Miss Susie M. Johnson
    *Lecture before the Society of Spiritualists,
    Oddfellows Hall, over the Post Office*
9. An Exposition of Spiritism
    Blanchard Hall, 233 S. Broadway
10. First Spiritualist Mission
    *Auxilliary State Spiritualist's Association,
    118-1/2 S. Spring Street*
11. Harmonial Spiritualist's Association
    *has secured permanent quarters in Broadway Central
    Hall, 121-1/2 S. Broadway*
12. Occult Spiritual Society
    *"Occult Phenomena," "Celestial Realms," Room 16,
    119-1/2 S. Spring Street*
13. First Spiritualist Church and School
    321 S. Hill
14. First Spiritualist Society (Incorporated)
    *Memorial Hall, I.O.O.F. building, 220-1/2 Main Street,
    "The Ethical & Spiritual Impact of Women's Suffrage"*
15. Concert and Select Dance
    *Given by the ladies of the First Spiritualist Society,
    ground floor, 216 W. Third Street. Entrance to hall
    through the storeroom of the Southern California
    Music Co., Third Street side of the Bradbury building*

Spiritualist Organizations and Activities in Los Angeles at the time of the Semi-Tropic Spiritualists, c. 1905-1910
www.semitropicspiritualists.com

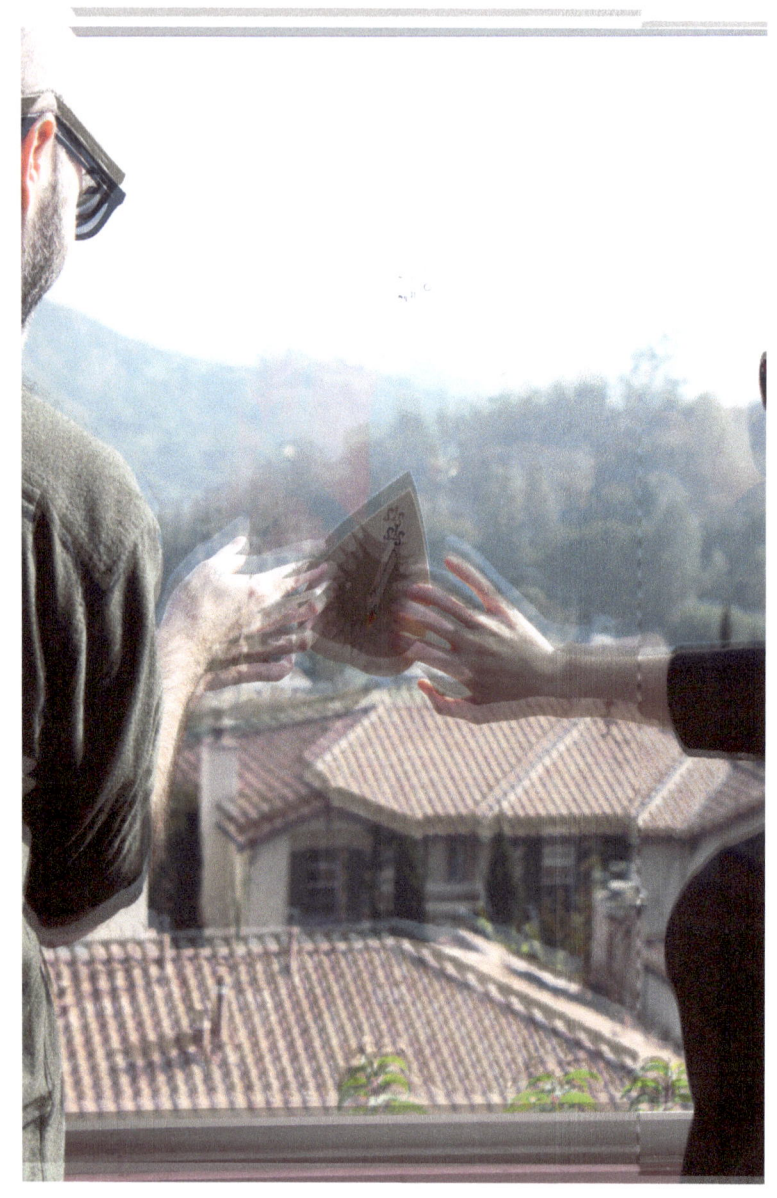

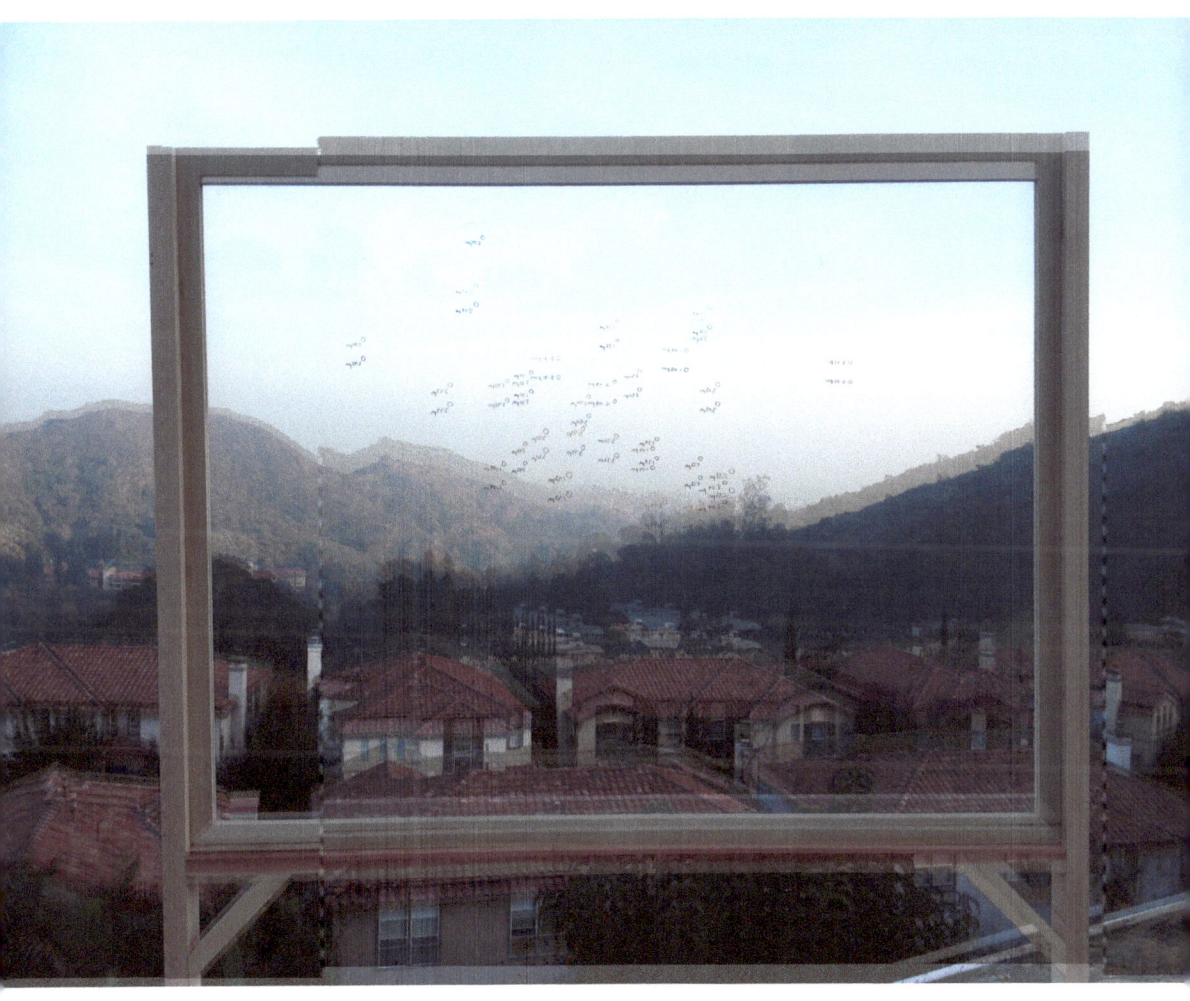

2.
Los Angeles
(present)

Semi-Tropic Spiritualist Test Site No. 2

Through studying the results of our first Test, we came to the realization that we are not looking for a single, physical place of spiritual energy, but rather, we seek to create a space for community, knowledge and investigation wherever we might find ourselves. Once we find a way to ground ourselves and establish a connection to the place where we are, each of us can be a locus for investigation. Like the camp meetings of the Semi-Tropic Spiritualists, where people were drawn together in the search for knowledge and community, we each have the capacity to build our own camp around ourselves.

In the spirit of the original Semi-Tropic Spiritualists, we continue their investigations and quest to create open spaces for community, knowledge and energy. Through the building of our fire, we re-establish their camp and join together as fellow investigators, always moving forward. Join us, as we build our fire where we stand.

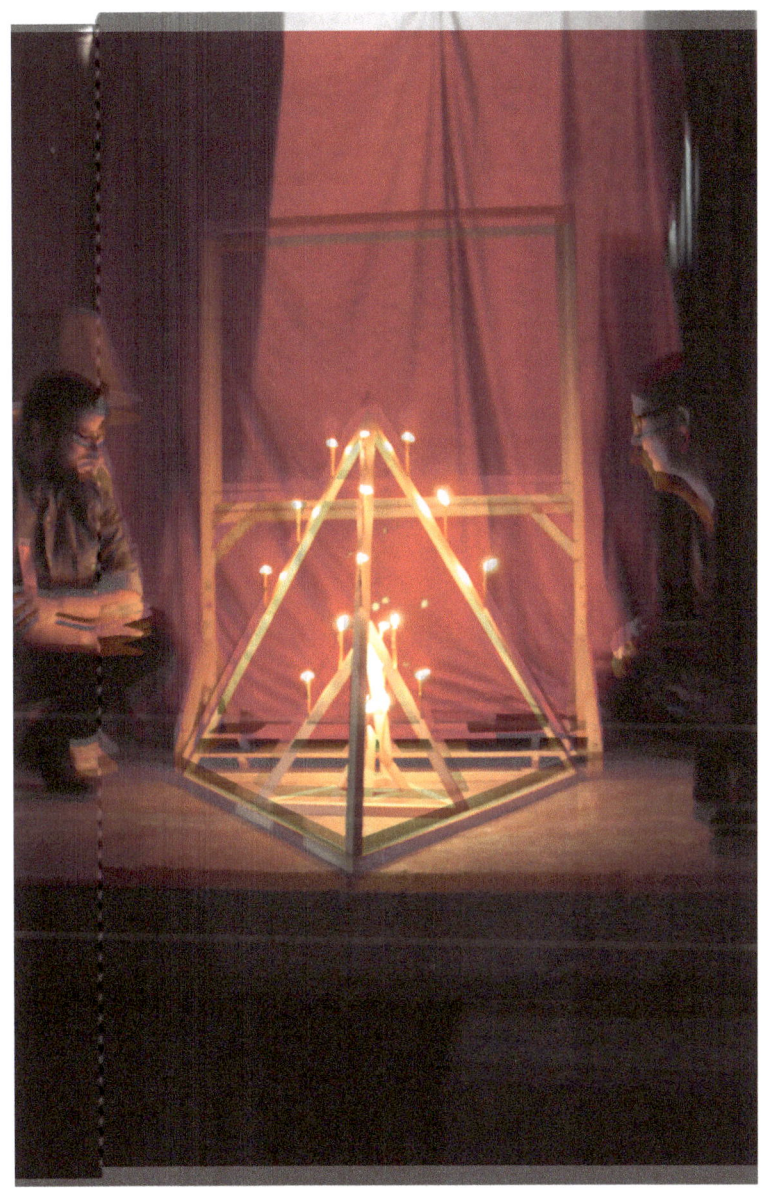

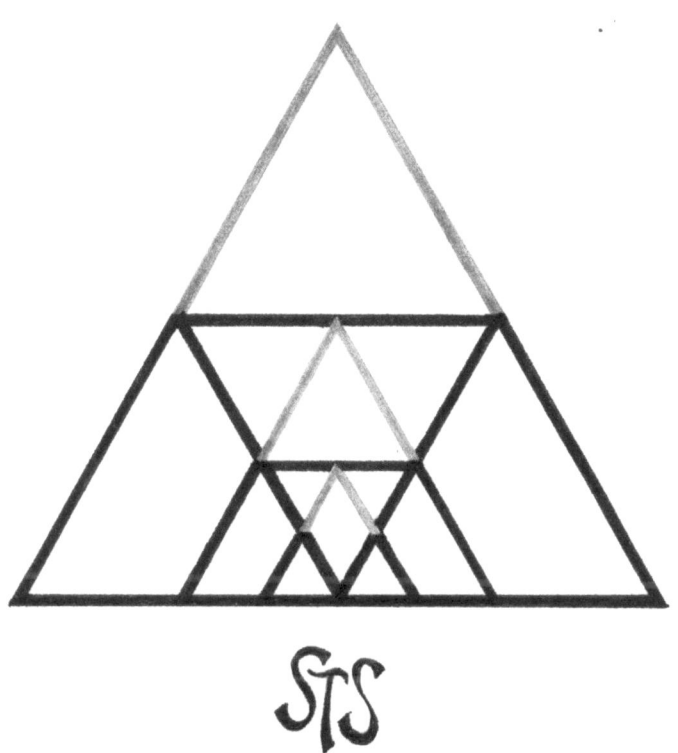

I: Hope and labor never faint;
    Weak misgivings banish,
When the heart is strong and clear,
    Obstacles will vanish:
Every effort, every hour,
    Nerves the worker with new power.

II: When each fulfills a wise design,
    In his own orbit he will shine.

III: Let us then be up and doing,
    With a heart for any fate:
Still acheiving, still pursuing,
    Learn to labor and to wait.

IV: Undepressed by seeming failure,
    Unelated by success;
Heights attained, revealing higher:
    Onward,
        Upward
    Ever press:

V. Deeply the miners will delve for gold,
   Regal wealth for us revealing;
   Wisdom has precious treasures untold,
   Ignorance is now concealing.

VI. Mysteries wondrous and grand unfold,
    In the onward march of ages:
    Slowly and surely time has unrolled
    Truth's illuminated pages.

VII. Wisdom has treasures greater far
     Than east or west unfold;
     And her rewards more precious are
     Than is the gain of gold.

VIII. Ever there floats before the real
      The bright, the beautiful ideal.

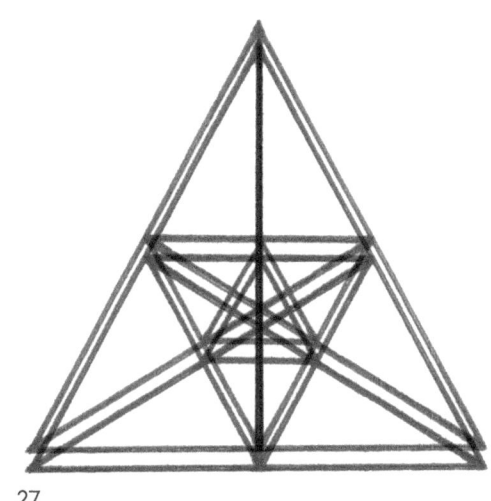

Semi-Tropic Spiritualists Test Site No. 2
Astri Swendsrud & Quinn Gomez-Heitzeberg
www.semitropicspiritualists.com

Quotations from Andrew Jackson Davis, <u>The Children's Progressive Lyceum: A Manual, with directions for the organization and management of Sunday Schools, adapted to the bodies and minds of the young, and containing rules, methods, exercises, marches, lessons, questions and answers, invocations, silver-chain recitations, hymns and songs, original and selected.</u> (1867)

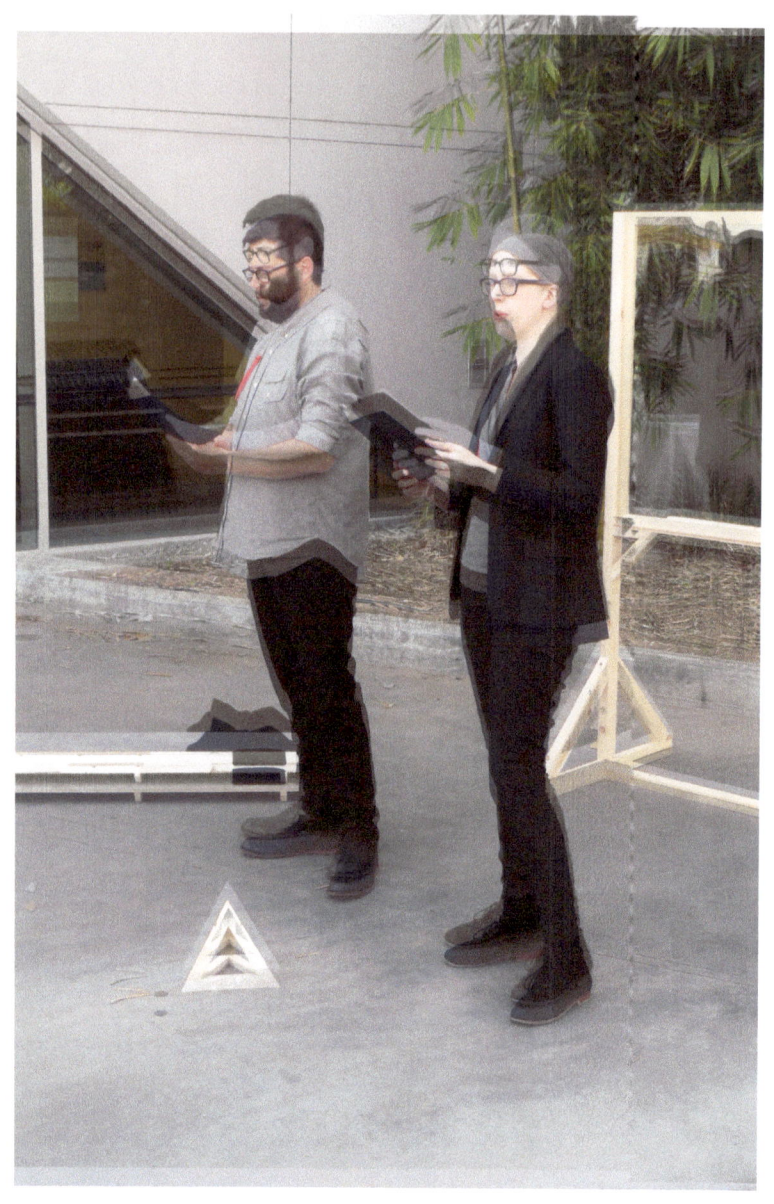

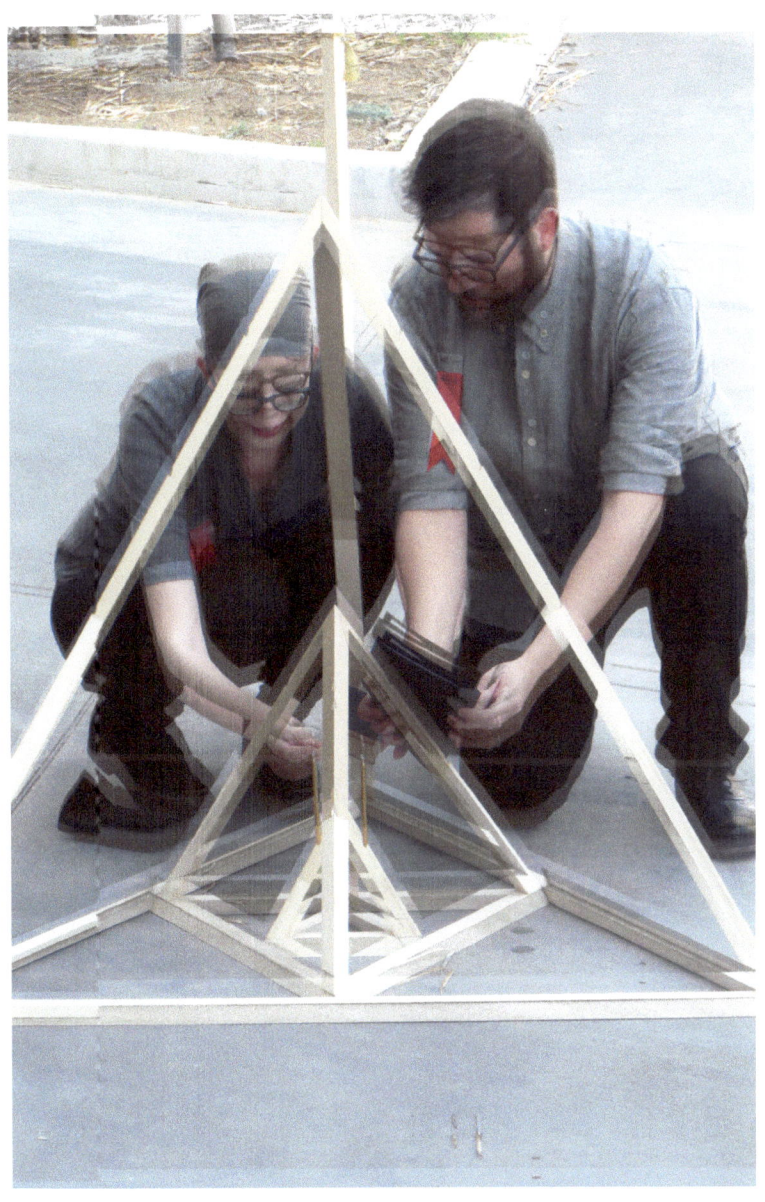

3.
Desert
(past)

Semi-Tropic Spiritualist Test Site No. 3

Inspired by the remote, desert landscape and the historical significance of open land as a place for experimental societies to flourish, we once again followed the lead of the original Semi-Tropic Spiritualist Association, traveling to the desert to create our own outpost in unoccupied territory. Surrounded by the ruins of Llano del Rio's utopian experiment, or within the undeveloped potential of the Joshua Tree landscape, we set up our tools of orientation. Our pendulum laid down a line, mapping east, back toward Spiritualism's origins in New York, and west to the Semi-Tropic Spiritualist's original camp site. Our campfire marked our temporary occupation.

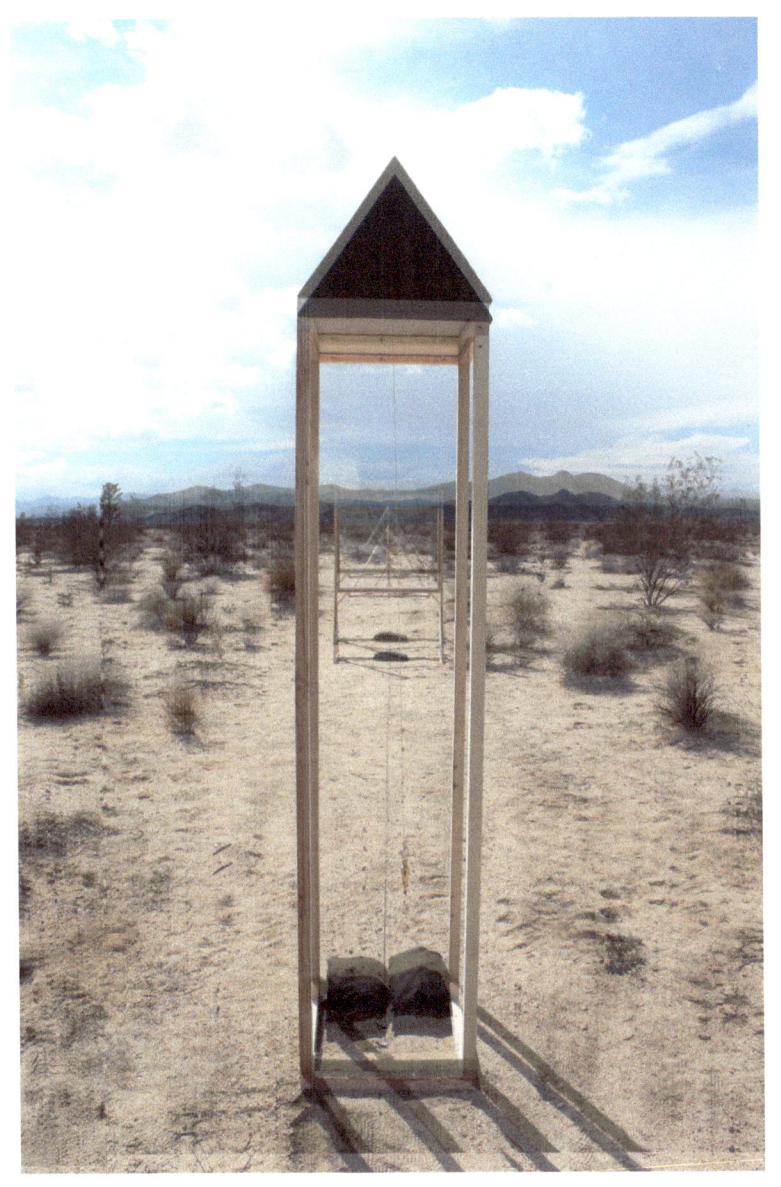

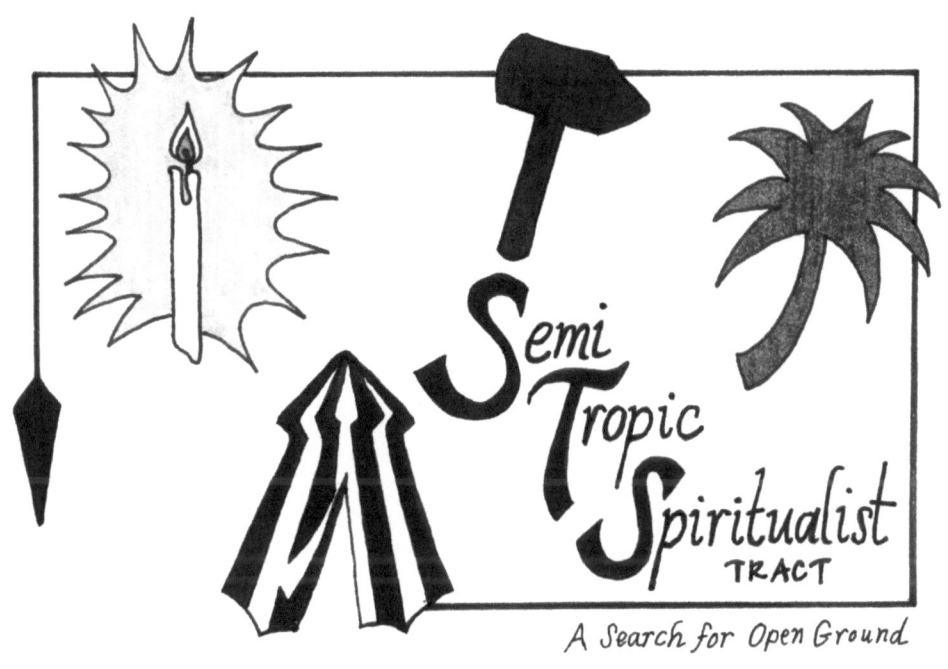

In 1905, the Semi-Tropic Spiritualist Association purchased a tract of land outside the city limits of Los Angeles. The tract was divided into small parcels for permanent dwellings, which surrounded a large central park. This park was set aside as a public meeting place for the Semi-Tropic Spiritualists to host camp meetings, including lectures, seances, investigations and tests.

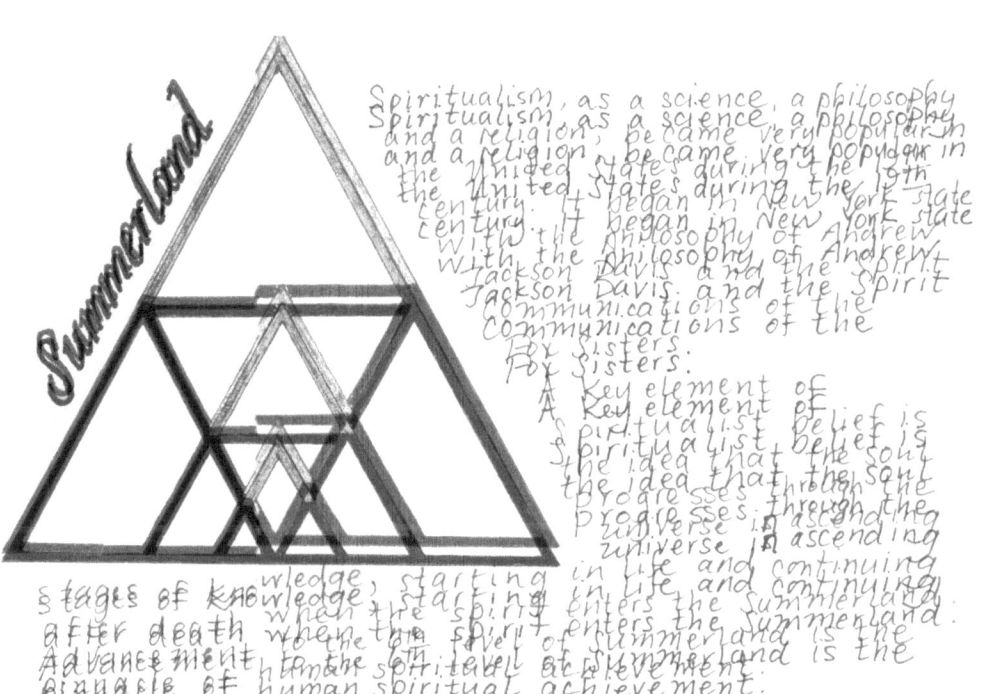

Spiritualism, as a science, a philosophy and a religion, became very popular in the United States during the 19th century. It began in New York state with the philosophy of Andrew Jackson Davis and the spirit communications of the Fox sisters.

A key element of spiritualist belief is the idea that the soul progresses through the universe in ascending stages of knowledge, starting in life and continuing after death when the spirit enters the Summerland. Advancement to the 6th level of Summerland is the pinnacle of human spiritual achievement.

As Spiritualism declined on the East Coast, many of its adherents traveled west to California to find a more open and progressive environment to practice and share their beliefs.

California

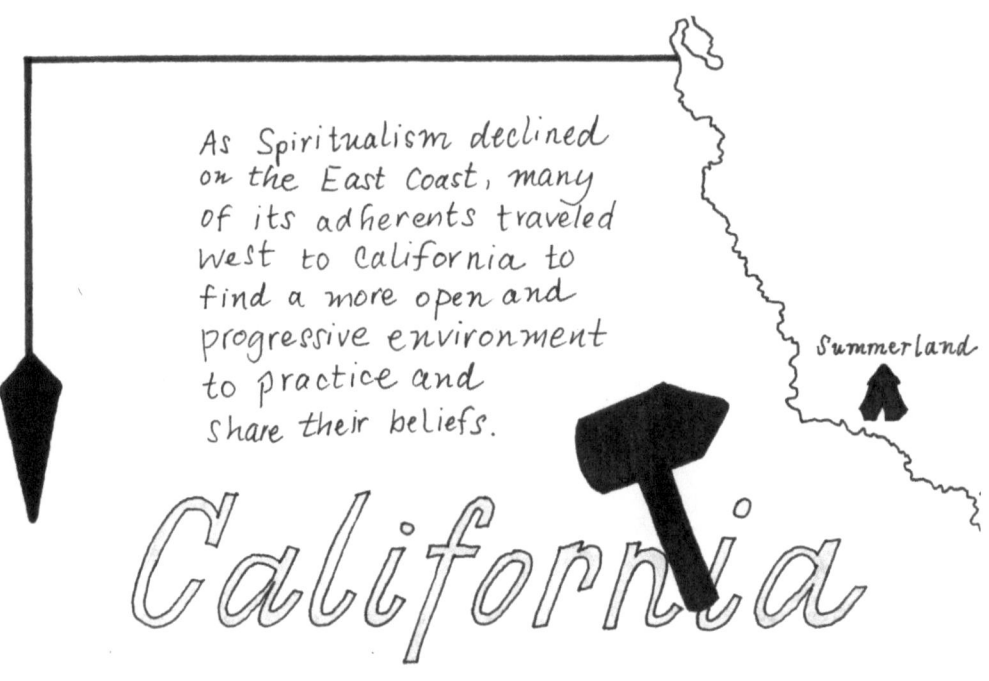

Summerland

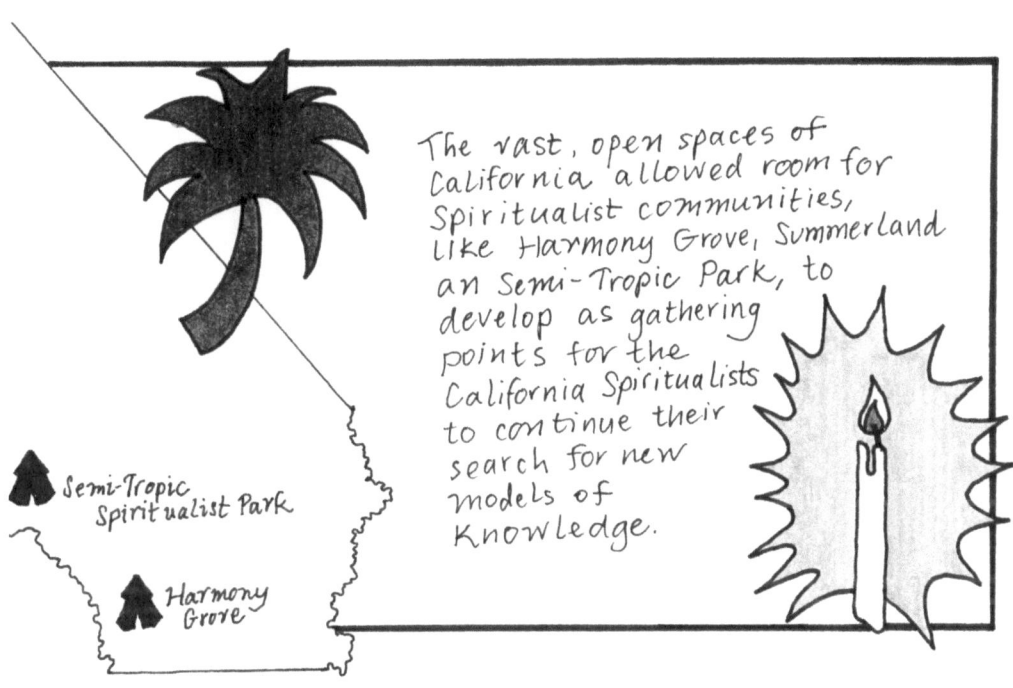

In the spirit of the original
Semi-Tropic Spiritualists,
we continue their investigations
and quest to create open
spaces for community,
knowledge and energy.
Through the building of
our fire, we re-establish
their camp and join
together as fellow
investigators; always
moving forward.

as we build our fire where we stand.
                  join us
                  join us

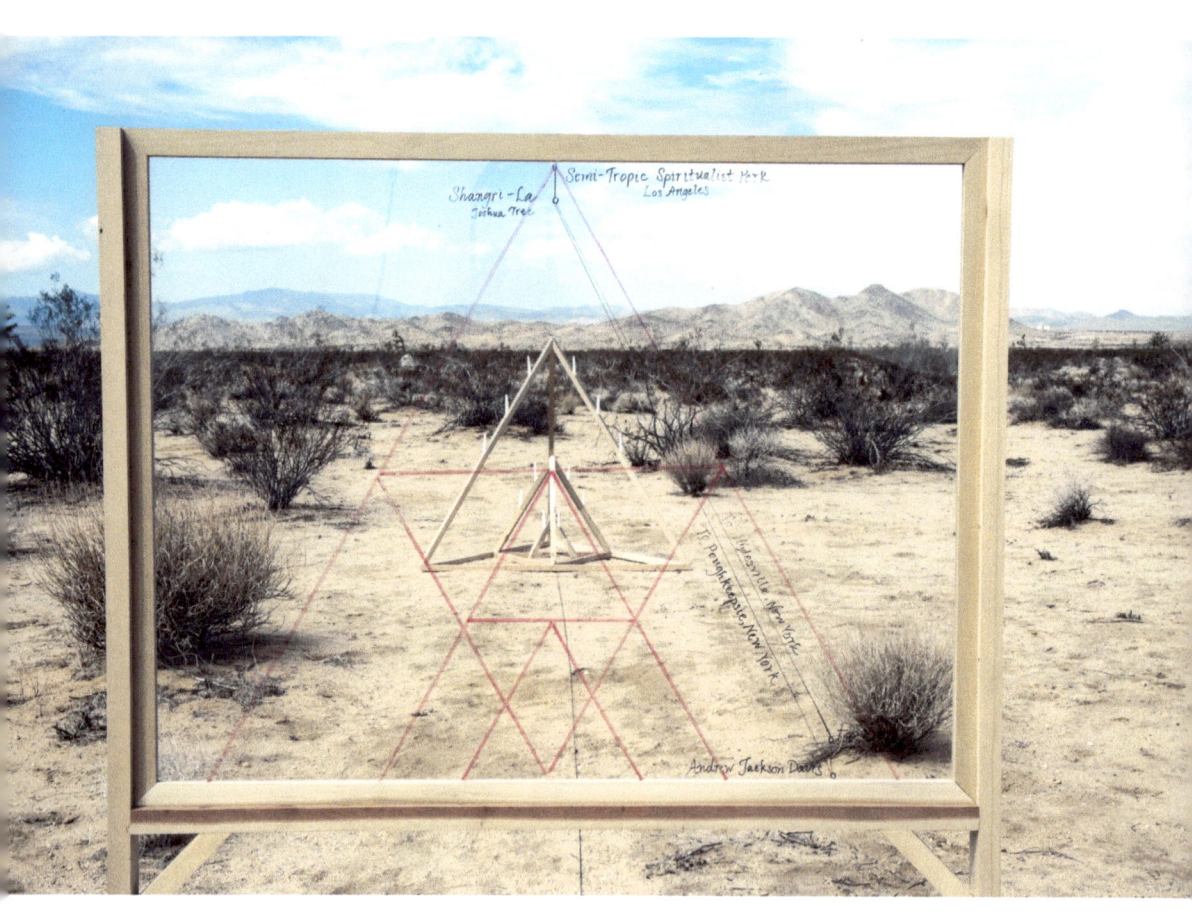

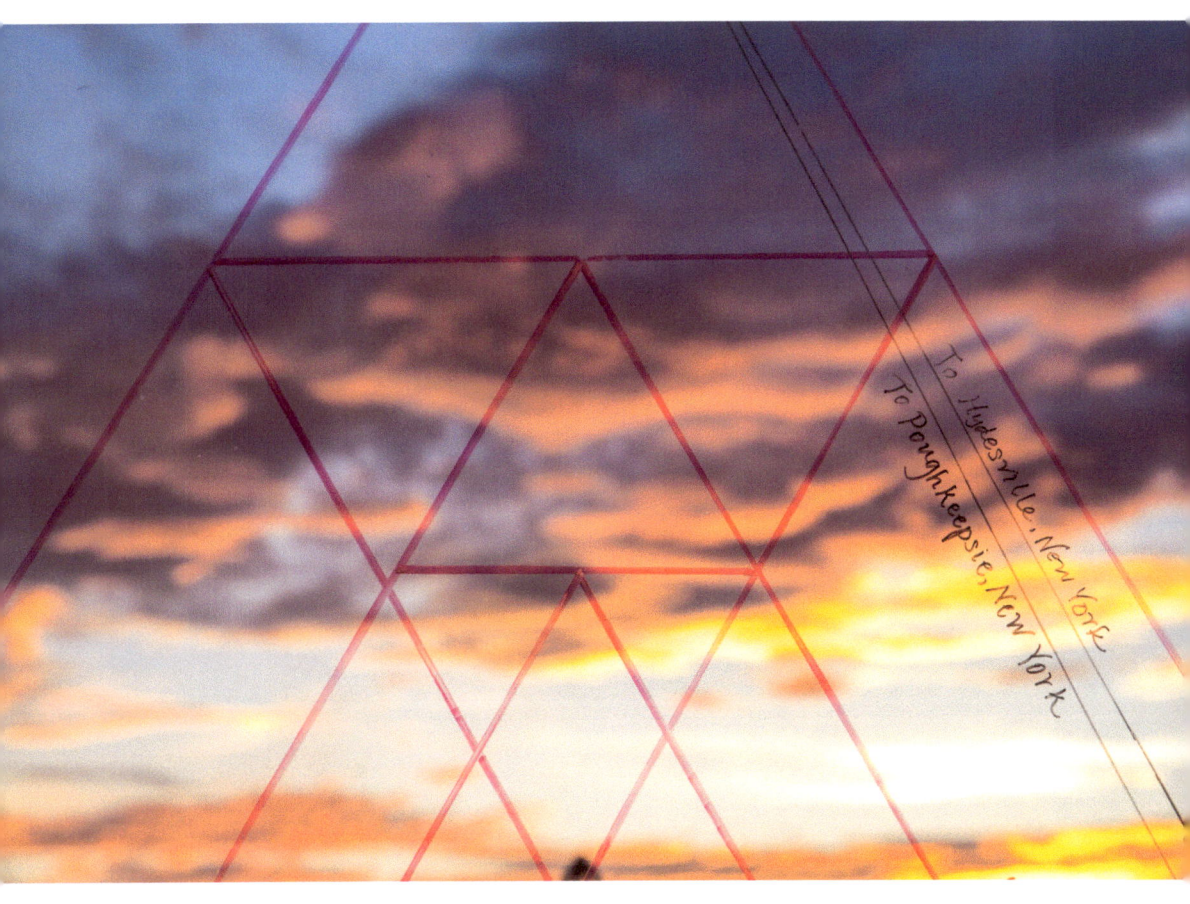

4: Los Angeles (present)

Semi-Tropic Spiritualist Test Site No. 4

The search for knowledge beyond the conscious mind has recurred, in various ways, throughout the history of Los Angeles. The Spiritualist camps of the early 1900s reappeared as the communes and alternative societies of the 1960s and 1970s, which have in turn lead to our re-establishing the Semi-Tropic Spiritualists alongside the seekers of today.

The historical practice of Spiritualism required no initial commitment of belief. Rather, it asked people to become investigators, to observe demonstrations of new phenomena and knowledge produced under test conditions in the séance room. The practice of a Spiritualist is a path of continuous exploration, guided by a philosophy of questioning. We wish to reconnect to our predecessors, to understand their quest in hopes of comprehending why we, along with so many others today, have returned to the same paths.

In questioning, we do not seek merely the answers of the conscious mind, but we desire to activate voices beyond our conscious reckoning. To facilitate us in this task, we have brought together a collection of objects through which to channel our responses. Our first instrument is the bell. Historically, bells and other musical instruments have been employed by mediums to reveal the unseen and the unheard. We seek to become attuned to the unspoken answers, the answers that lie beyond our immediate recognition, as signaled by our bells. Our second tool is a deck of cards made up of six images, which contain the symbolism of the Semi-Tropic Spiritualists. These symbols represent the major themes and questions of our endeavor.

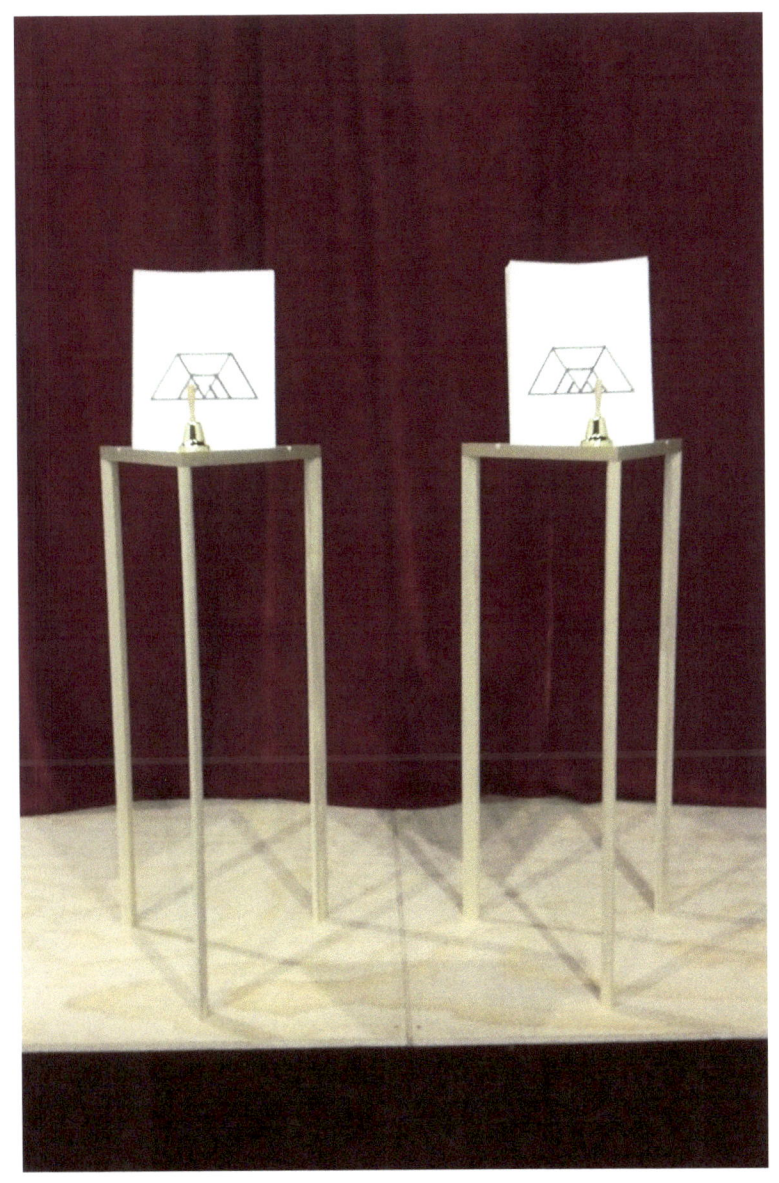

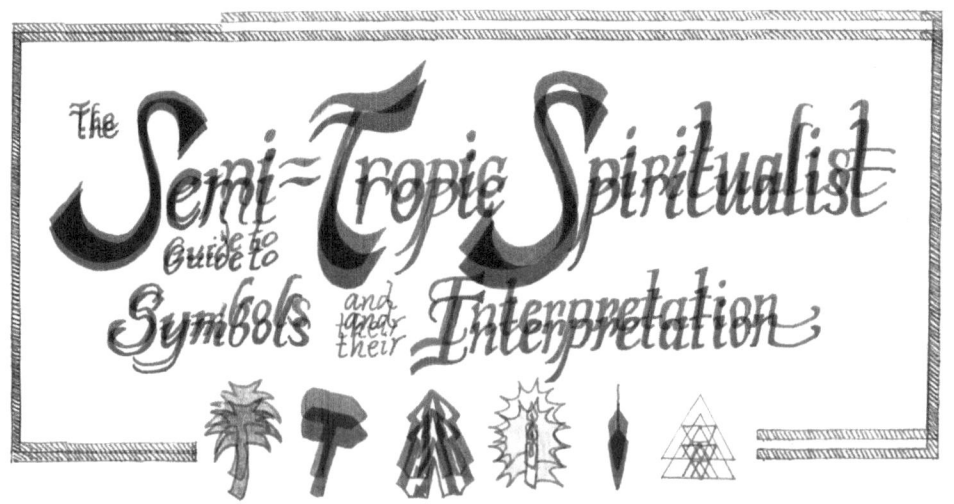

Spontaneous and profound questions
desires; but to obtain and enjoy
which are intrinsically elevating
consult, not superficial and popular
and unchangeable teaching of

are living representatives of internal those pure and beautiful responses, and eternal, the inquirer must authorities, but the everlasting Nature, Reason and Intuition.

—Andrew Jackson Davis

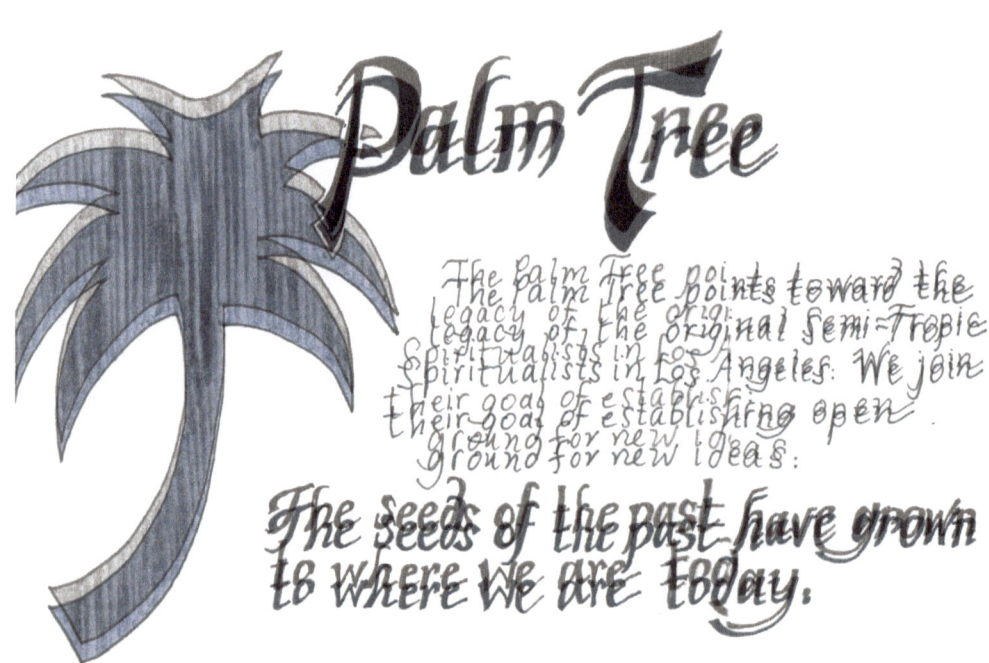

Palm Tree

The Palm Tree points toward the legacy of the original Semi-Tropic Spiritualists in Los Angeles. We join their goal of establishing open ground for new ideas.

The seeds of the past have grown to where we are today.

The Hammer represents our labor, work and effort as we seek to carry out the Semi-Tropic Spiritualists aims. This quest for knowledge is an active endeavor, as we work to lay the foundation for our camp.

The camp will only stand if the stakes are driven deeply.

Hammer

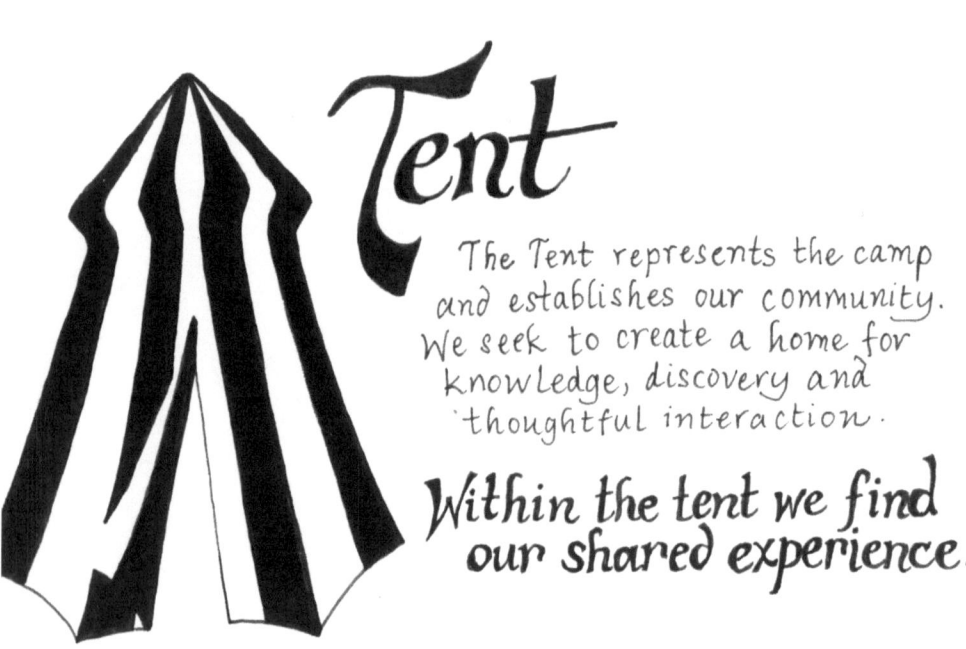

Tent

The Tent represents the camp and establishes our community. We seek to create a home for knowledge, discovery and thoughtful interaction.

Within the tent we find our shared experience.

The candle is the fire of knowledge. It represents the goals of learning and enlightenment that guide all we do.

Our fire illuminates the path before us.

Candle

Pendulum

The Pendulum signifies the unknown that is encountered on the path of questioning. We are not fearful of the unknown, for from it we divine new directions to explore.

With our pendulum we plumb the space beyond our knowledge.

The Triple Pyramid represents Summerland, the ultimate goal and culmination of spiritualist philosophy. The path is one of continuous exploration, guided by constant questioning.

Our knowledge ascends through this life and beyond.

Triple Pyramid

Man must both desire and learn to
power to ask. But what questions
Who shall answer? We must
Come then, ye children of experience,
And the world will accept all the

answer every question he finds the
now appear? Who shall ask?
have no more dogmatism!
let us hear your words: speak!
truth ye can give.

— Andrew Jackson Davis

5: The Hatchery

Semi-Tropic Spiritualist Test Site No. 5

The impetus for this Test Site stems from a physical site of recurring alternative societies – The Hatchery, located near the small town of Badger in Central California.

In 1958, Synanon was founded in Santa Monica, California to help drug addicts find a path of recovery and transformation. In 1970, when Synanon moved to the mountain compound called The Hatchery, their reach had broadened to include all those seeking tools to re-structure their lives within an alternative society. In 1996, Baladullah also came to The Hatchery to create a religious community of peaceful refuge and education.

The Semi-Tropic Spiritualists, Synanon, and Baladullah each began as an experiment in finding a better way of being in the world. Utopias begin with a plan, and the belief that the right plan can lead to a more perfect community. However, the actualization of an ideal–moving from the two-dimensional, perfect plan to the three-dimensional, imperfect world–always creates complications. Both Synanon and Baladullah's perfect social plans ultimately could not be sustained within reality.

Synanon's alternative society collapsed from within. What began with a promise of therapeutic transformation became a system of violence, aggression and abuse, under the control of a totalitarian leader. Although Baladullah began as a haven to escape the pressures of the outside world, it was unable to remove itself from external conflicts. Baladullah fell in the wake of September 11, to suspicion and public fear of an isolated, Islamic community. The Hatchery site was then abandoned and has remained empty to this day.

Even in the face of the disillusionment and failure that such examples represent, we seek to remain free of cynicism and maintain hope for new possibilities of living. The Semi-Tropic Spiritualists traveled to The Hatchery in order to take its collapse of utopia back to a place of potential. We must undo in order to rebuild. We came to extinguish the candle, to unbuild the fire, to clean the slate.

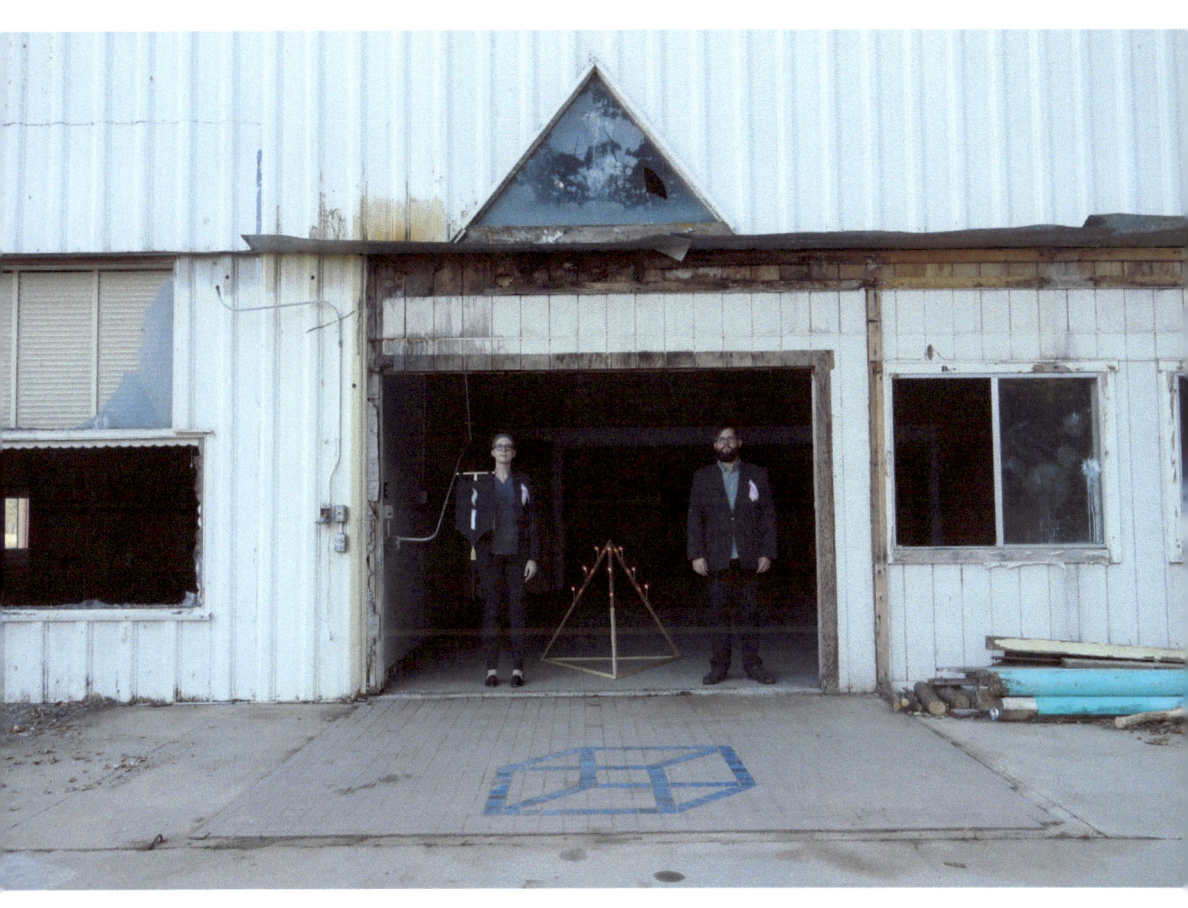

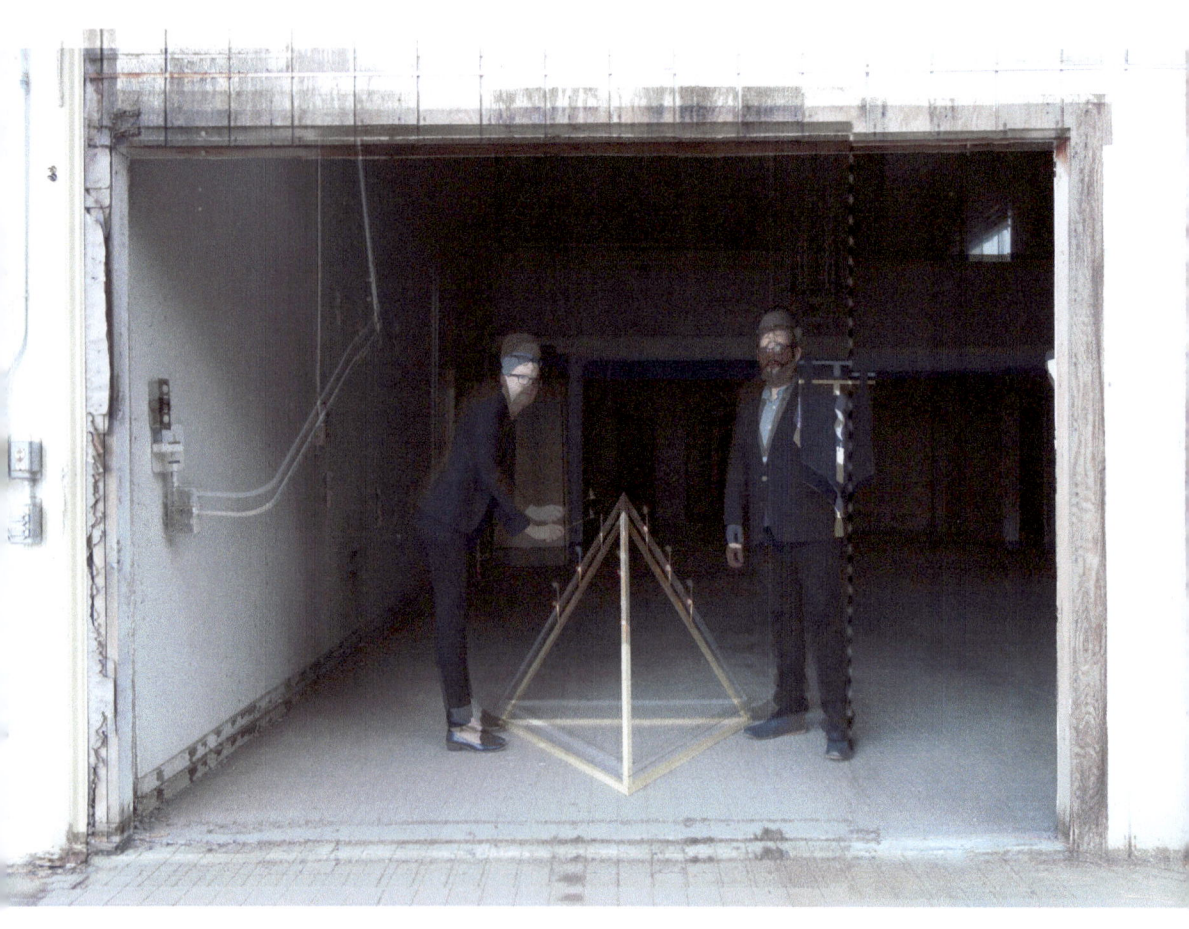

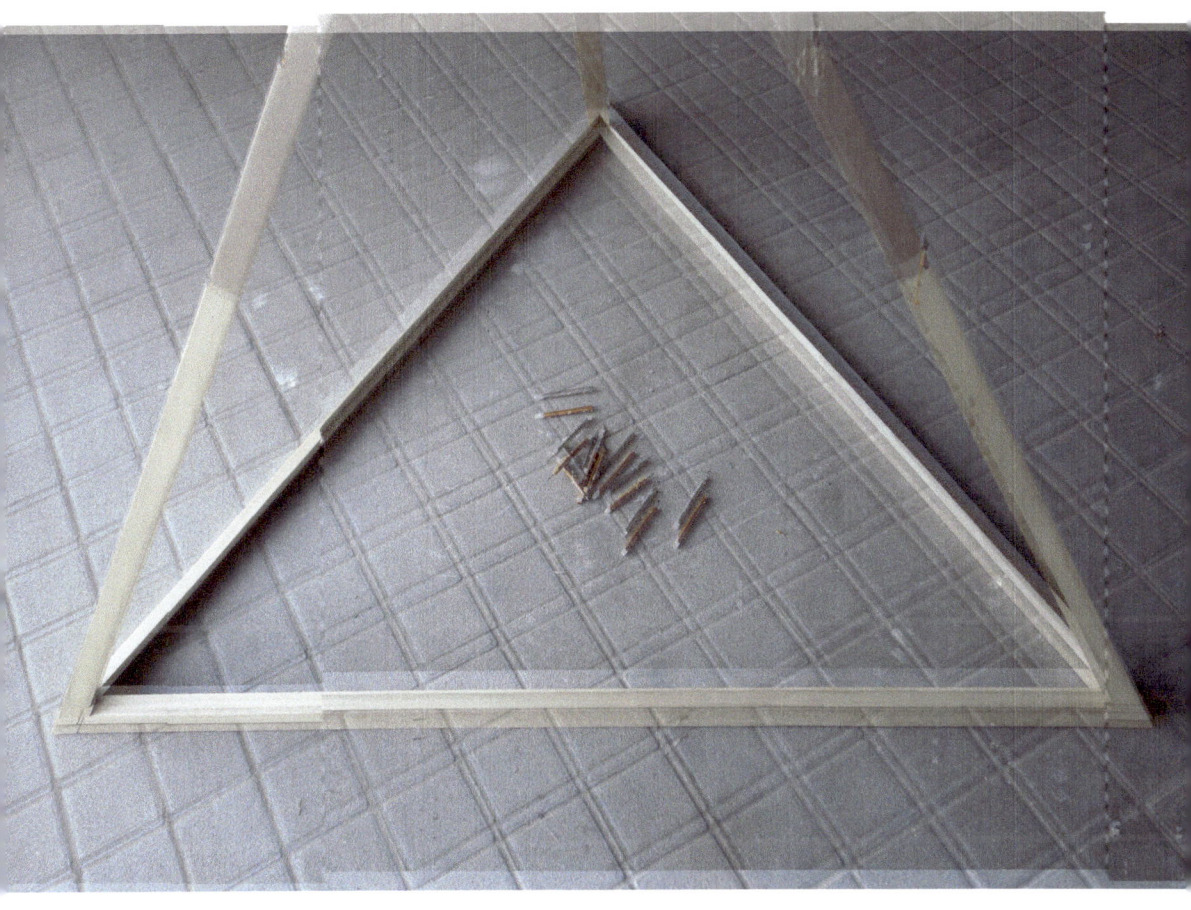

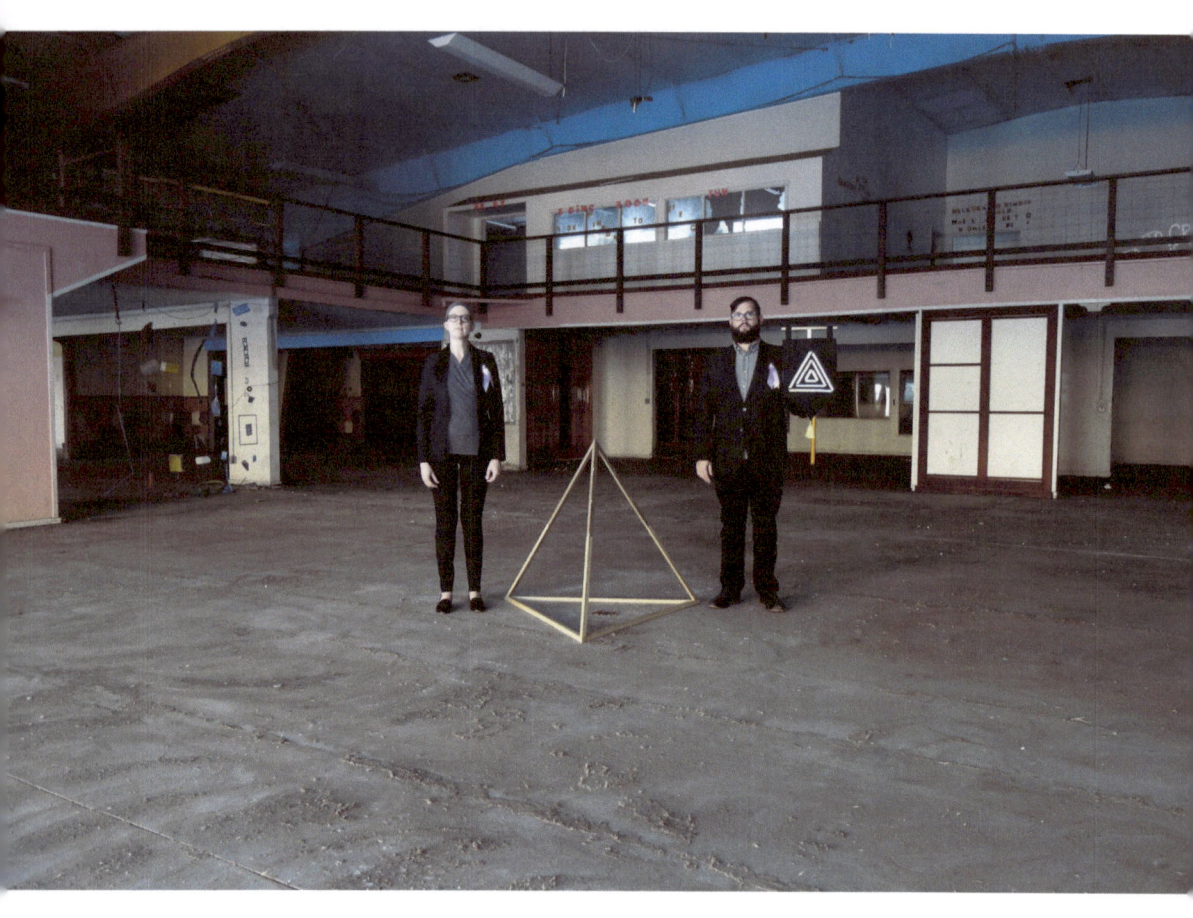

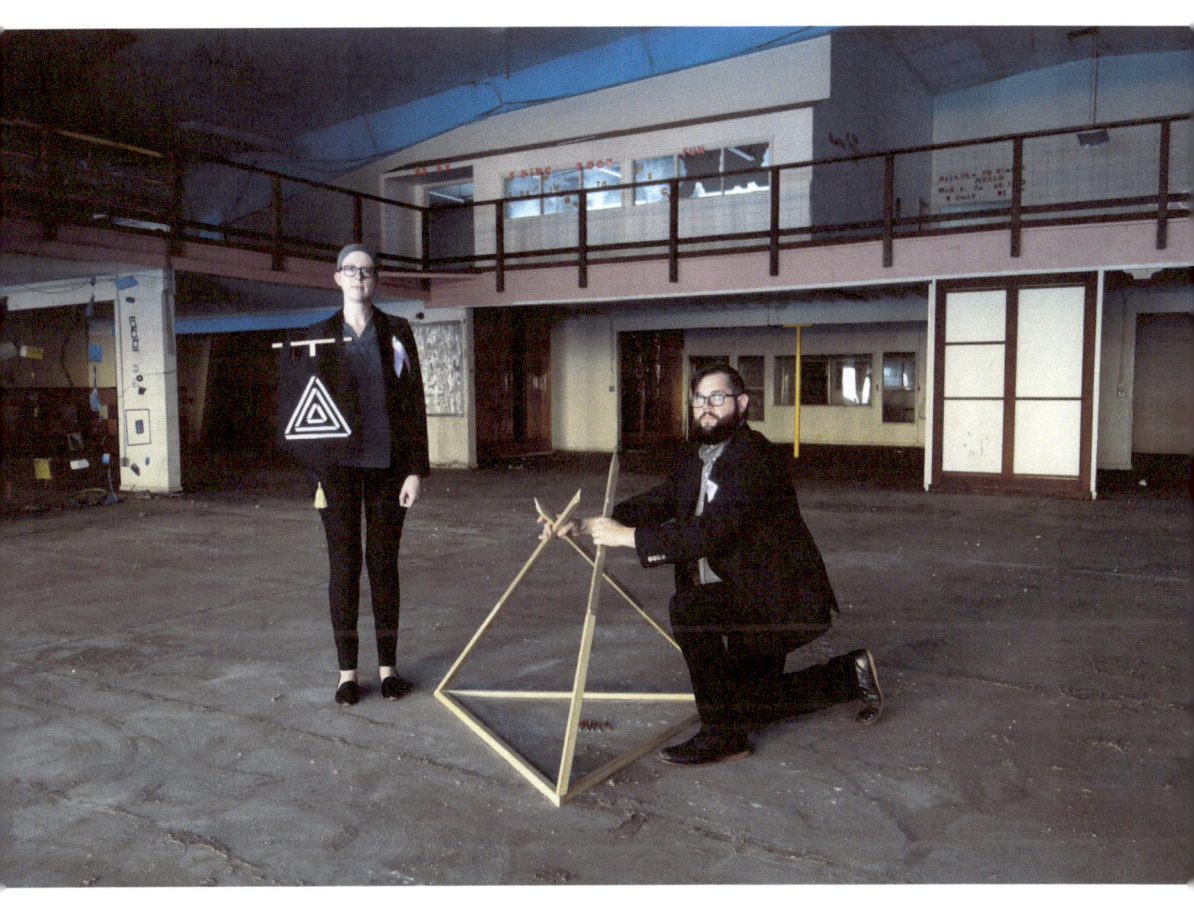

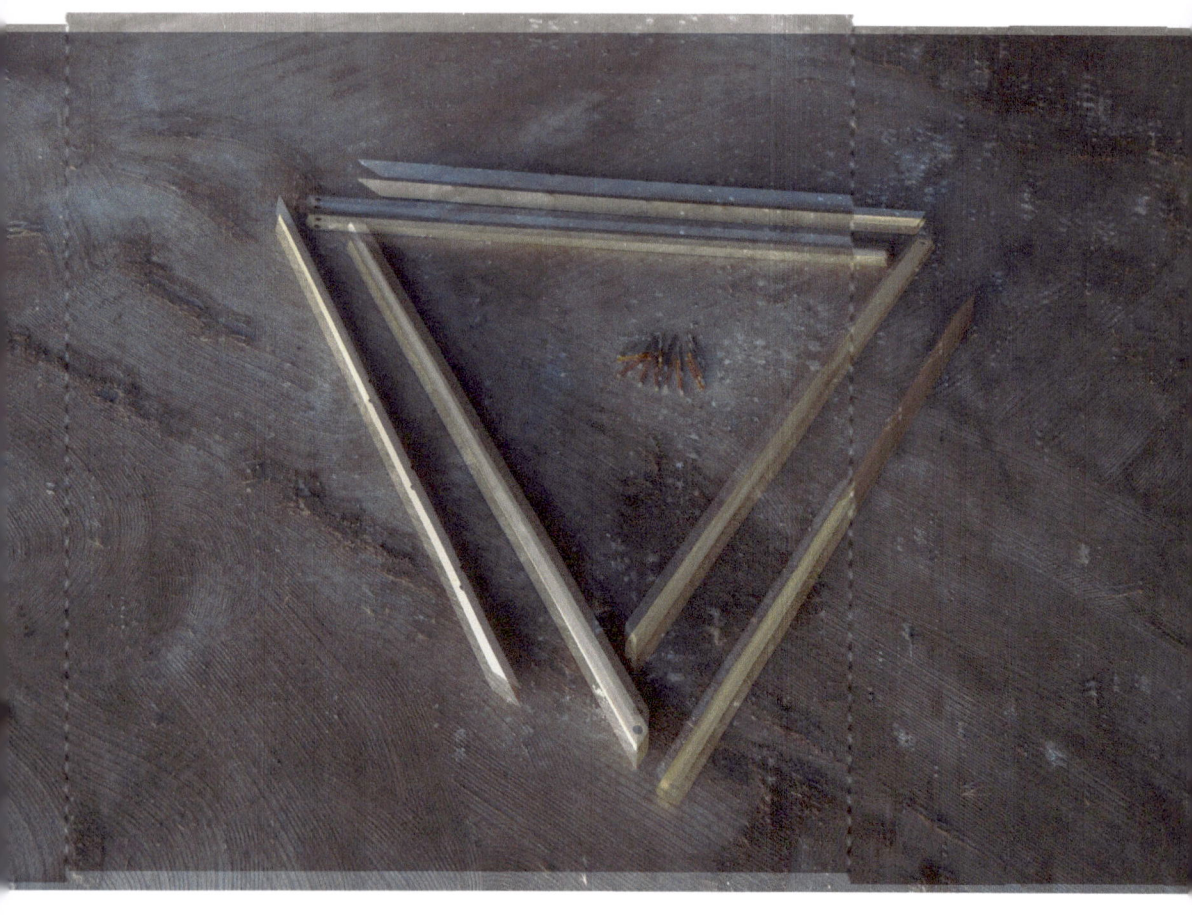

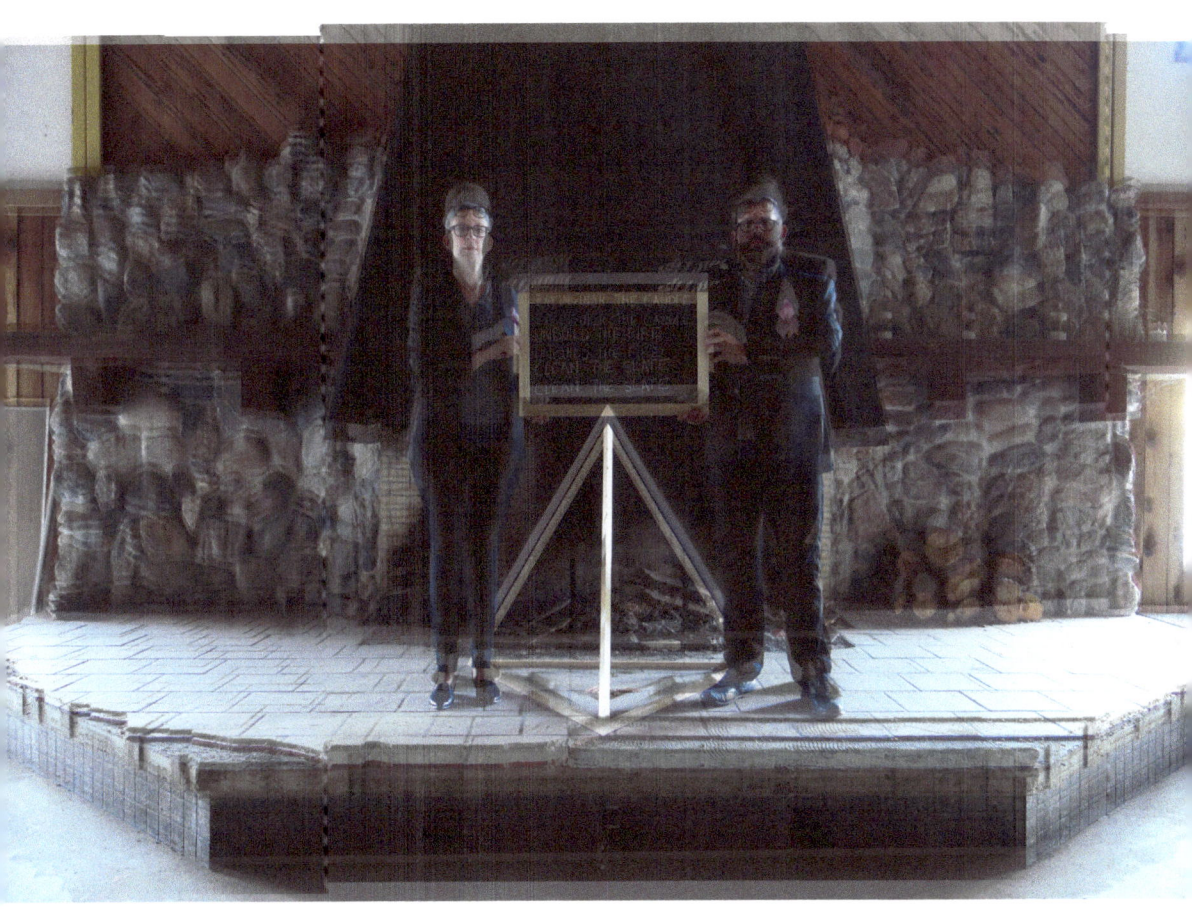

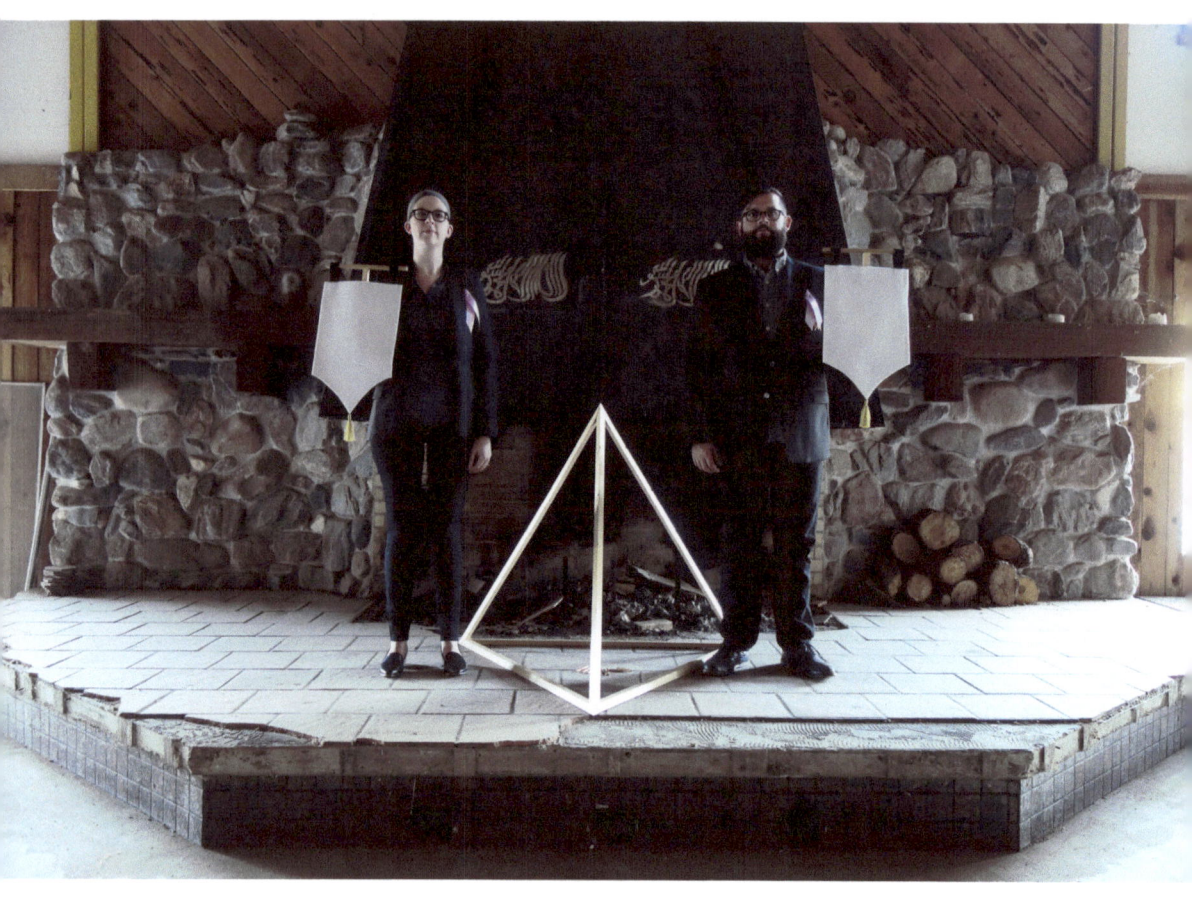

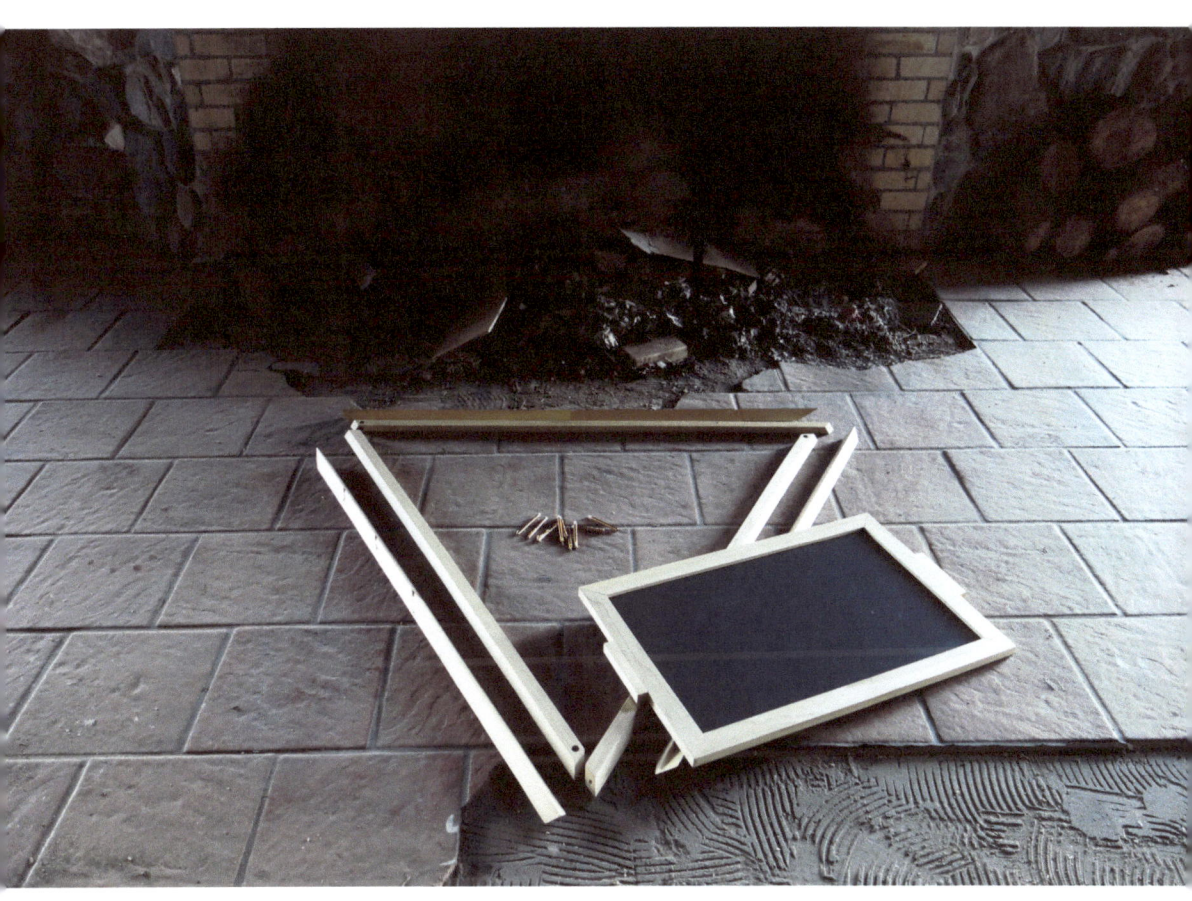

6: Irvine

Semi-Tropic Spiritualist Test Site No. 8

Our investigations are guided by a path of questioning, as we seek out places of alternative social possibility and new models for being in the world. For this Test Site, our path lead us to Irvine, California. Irvine's noteworthy present-day status didn't evolve from happenstance. It's the outcome of master planners, and those engaged to institute the plan.

In the 1960s, William Perieira and the Irvine Company designed a Master Plan for the city that we saw around us. This plan was meant to guide the orderly development of the entire Irvine Ranch. Inside these expanding geometries of community and commerce, Perieria and the Irvine Company envisioned a built environment that could shape both a space and the lives within it toward a successful future. We brought our tools—our pendulums, used by both surveying city-planners and divining mystics—to test the boundaries of this space.

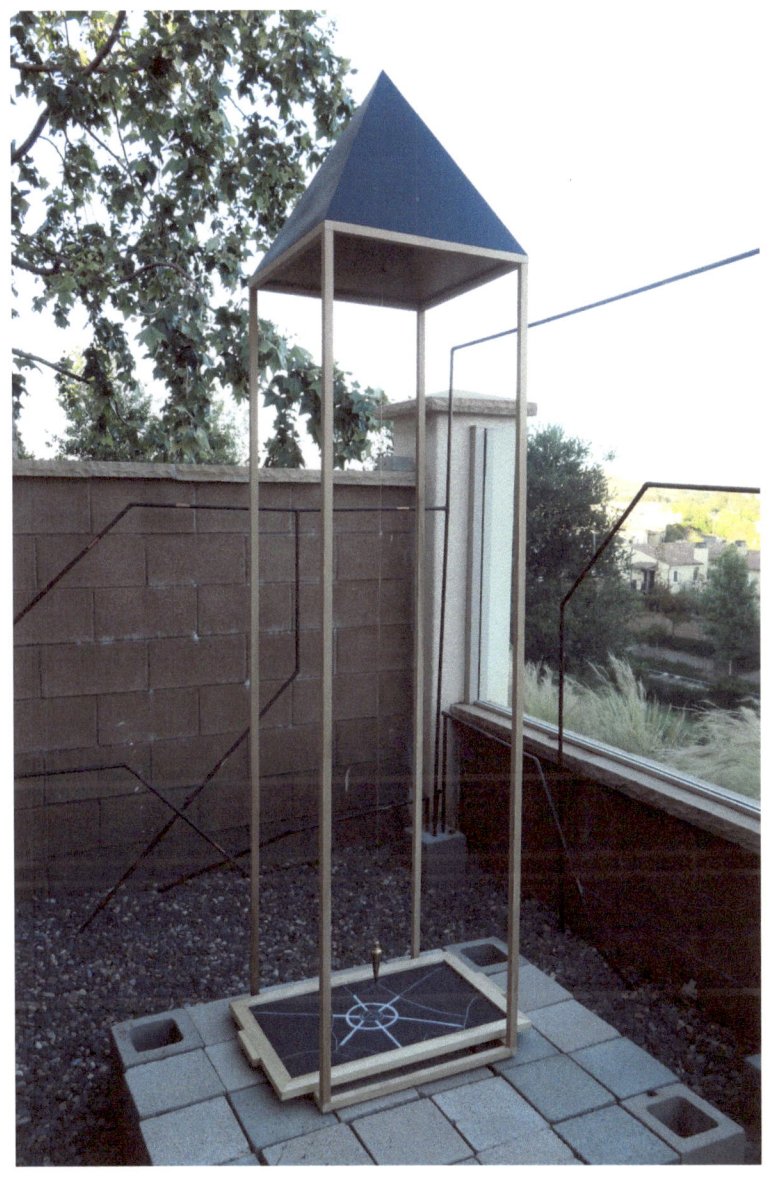

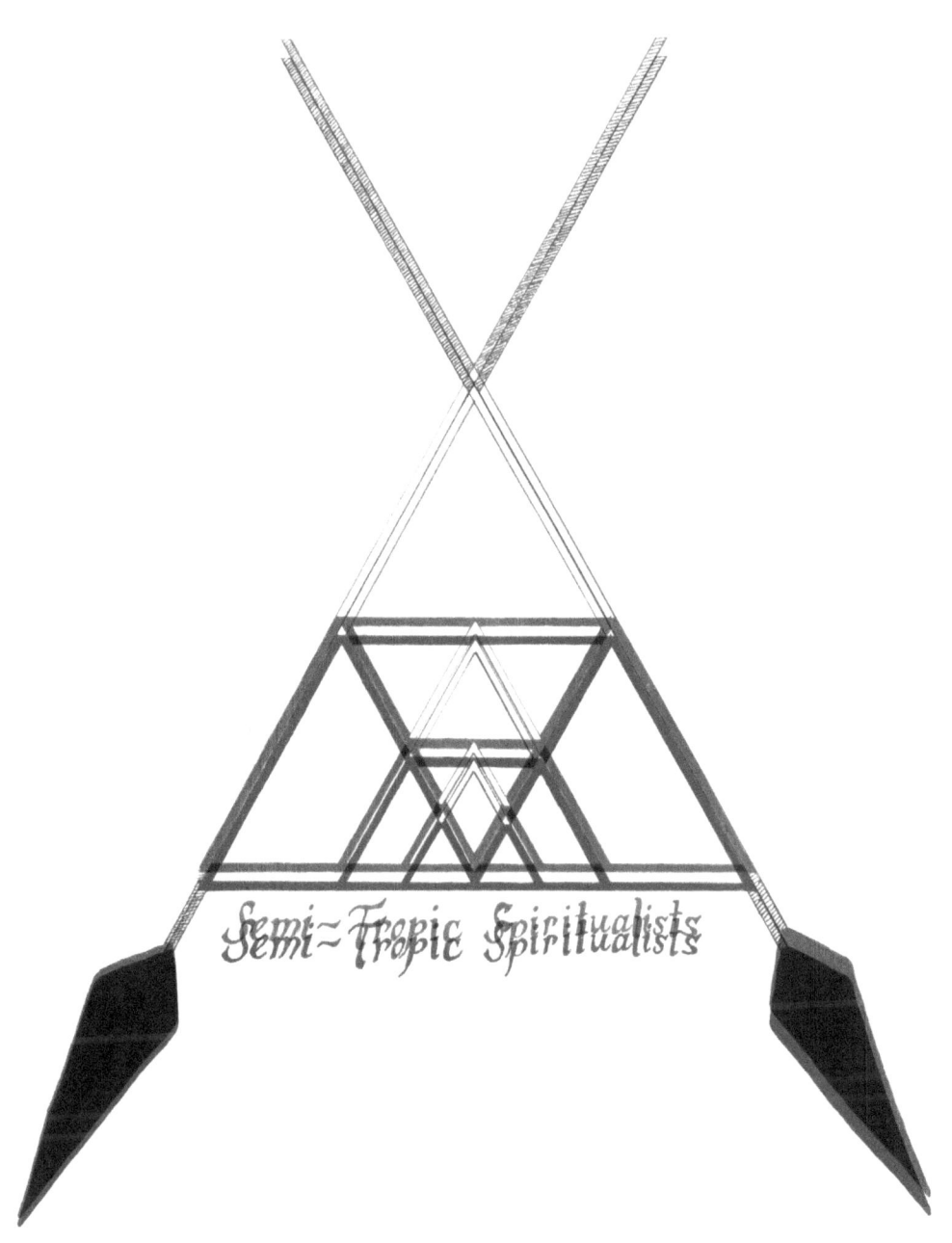

*The Surveyors plumb the land,
The Diviners seek the unknown,*

I. From the Surveyors comes the Plan —
   finding potential within the spaces of our world.

II. From the Surveyor's Plan our reality is built —
   ideas taking form and shaping the boundaries of our lives.

III. From the Surveyor's Plan grows a community —
   together we occupy the spaces and roles laid out for us.

and build the world around us.
and reveal what lays beyond us.

VI. The Diviner continues ever forward~
as our knowledge ascends through
this life and beyond.

V. The Diviner moves from one question to the next~
following the path that leads to enlightenment.

IV. From the Diviner comes the questions~
we move beyond the plan to see where the
unknown takes us.

The Surveyors came to this place to develop an idea. They looked at the open expanse of land and they created The Plan. This Plan was formed in a spirit of optimism, designing a map to guide the future of this space toward the most desirable outcomes of safety and prosperity.

It is not enough to simply have The Plan. In order for The Plan to become truly meaningful, it must be put into practice. The Surveyor's ideas were built into spatialized, physical form. The streets, neighborhoods, homes, and businesses around us were all built according to the boundaries laid out by The Plan. These structures define the space of possibility for those within their borders.

Within the physical space laid out by The Surveyors, a community is established. Individual lives are brought together within the spaces defined by The Plan, within the structures designed for a comfortable existence. This community works according to The Plan, manifesting its ideals together as long as we follow its guidance.

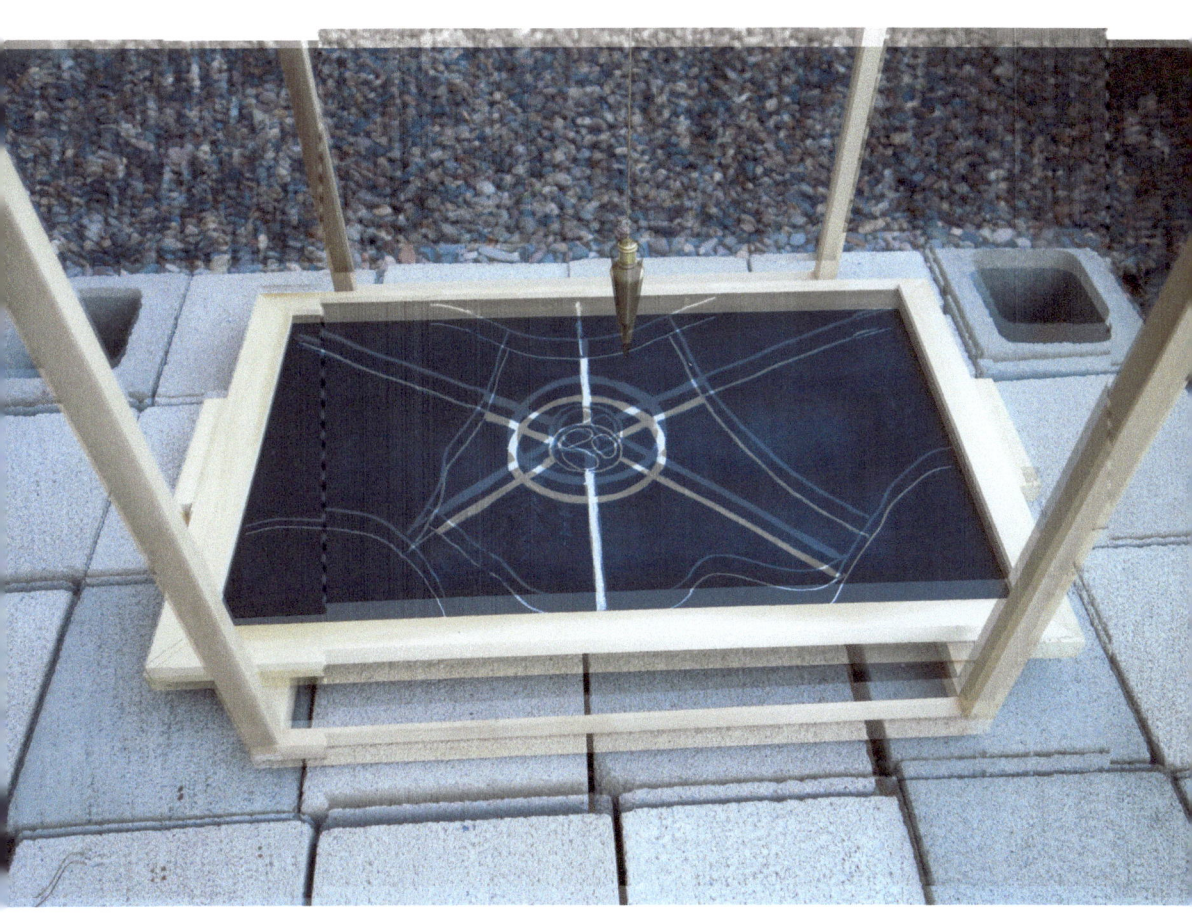

The community is at once The Plan's greatest achievement and its greatest challenge. Within The Plan's boundaries and controls, where is there space for the unknown, the individual, all the variables that do not fit or cannot be anticipated by The Plan? It is here that the Surveyor needs to invite the collaboration of The Diviner. The Diviner welcomes the mystery, looking with anticipation into the space beyond our knowledge.

Following the lead of The Diviner's questions, we are able to move into a path of learning and enlightenment. This process of discovery allows us to perceive the limitations of The Plan and opens up avenues for expanded exploration. The new and the unknown can be uncomfortable spaces to occupy, but it's only through this quest for knowledge that new ideas and new possibilities can come into being.

The path of the Diviner moves ever forward – a process of continuous exploration, guided by constant questioning. The Surveyors would never have come to The Plan if they had not been first moving through the world as Diviners, seeking new possibilities. Let us not become so comfortable following the Surveyor's Plan that we forget to activate the Diviner's pendulum. Only then can we continue ascending.

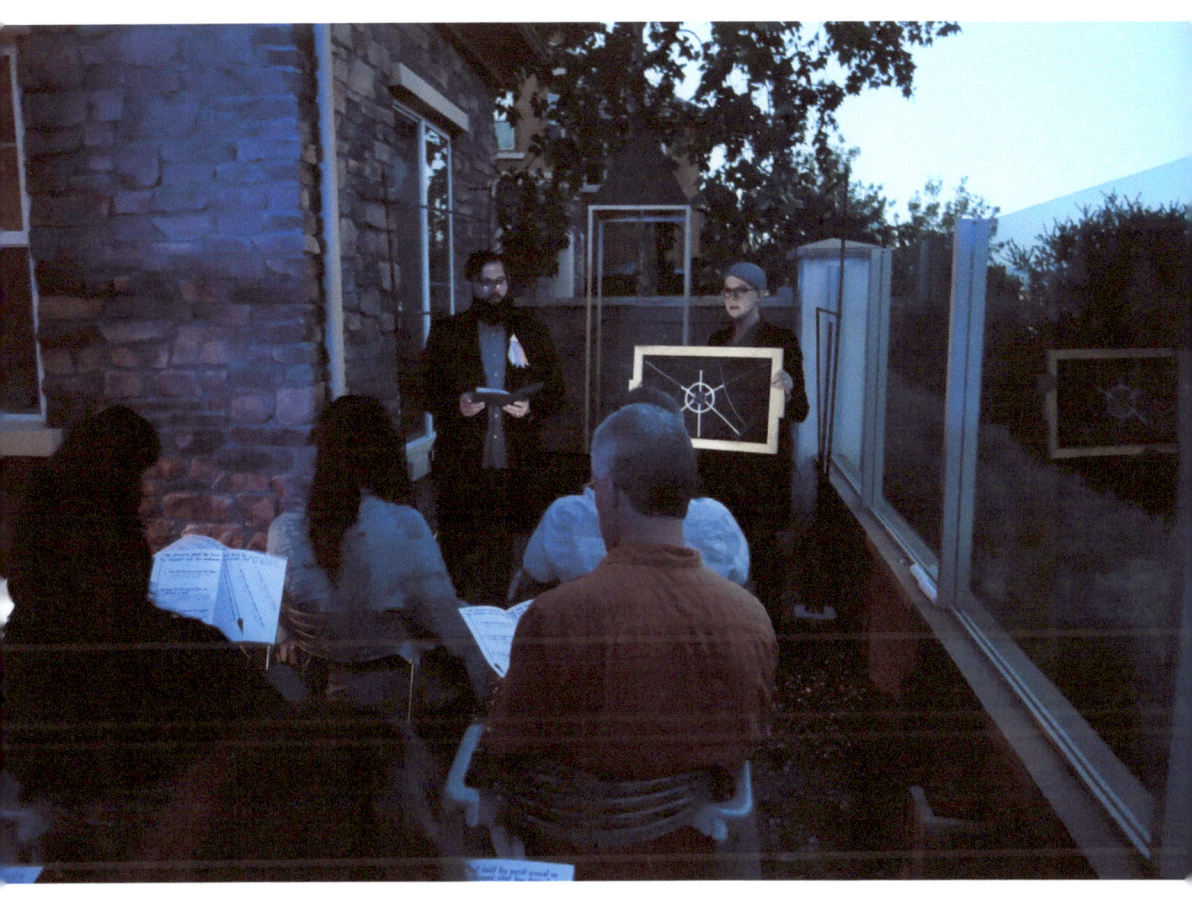

7. Desert (present)

Semi-Tropic Spiritualist Test Site No. 6

In the years since the founding of the Semi-Tropic Spiritualists, the site of our camp has been lost to development. Although we may not be able to return to the physical location where the original Semi-Tropic Spiritualists once walked, we can still follow in their paths.

To aid in this endeavor we traveled to this site of potential, where we have brought together a collection of relics gathered from our past. Though it may be impossible to fully return to our original campsite, we can use these objects to connect with our ideals – through the memory, energy, and attention that accumulates around them by our use and contemplation. The relics you see are physical reminders of where we have come from. They are the actual objects that we have used in our effort to re-establish the Semi-Tropic Spiritualists today. However, these objects have also come to symbolize our ideals. They point not only to the past, but pose questions regarding where we will go next.

We also brought with us dirt gathered from the site where the Semi-Tropic Spiritualist camp once stood. This dirt contains a history of idealism, of a community in search of new ways of thinking and being. We will take this dirt and, carrying it as a community, walk through this pilgrimage of our ideals and our reality.

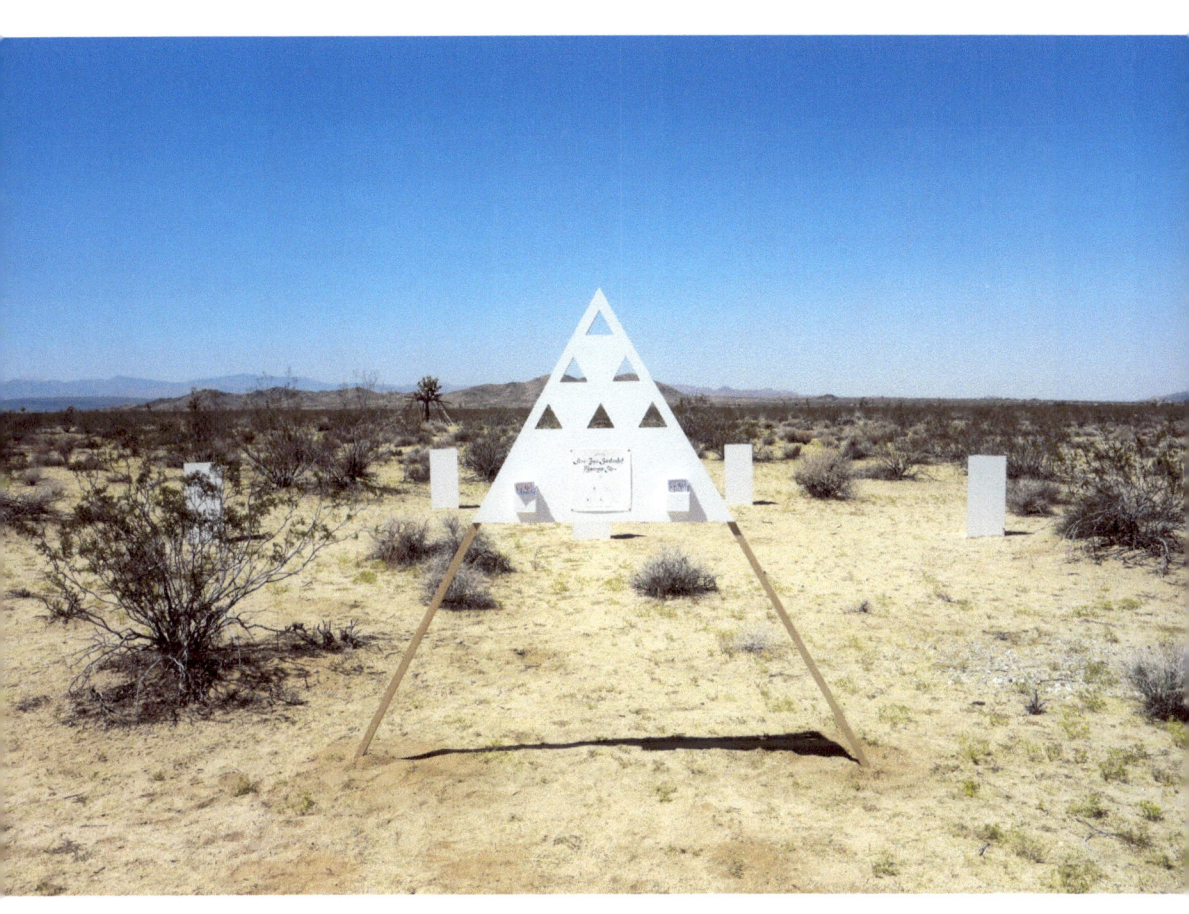

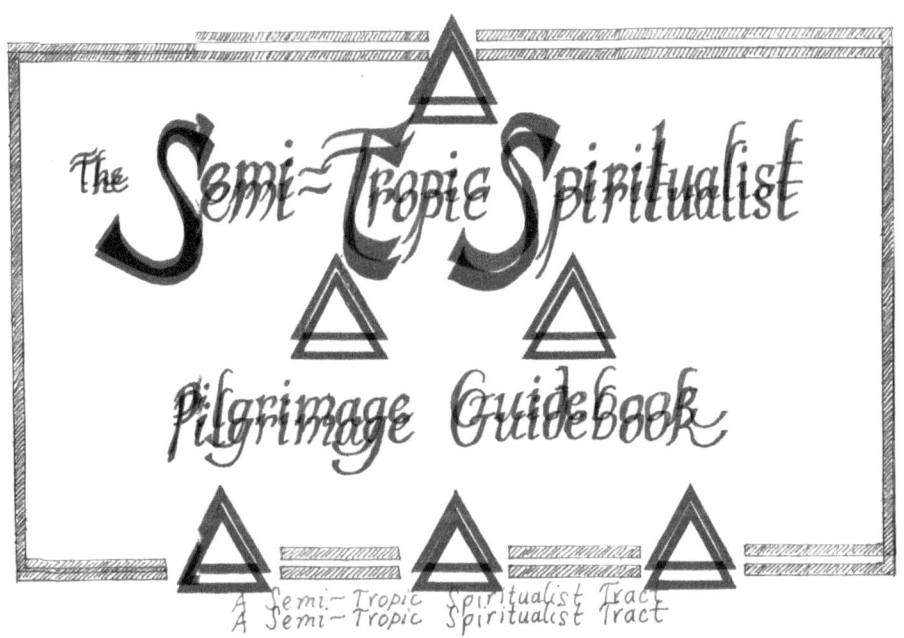

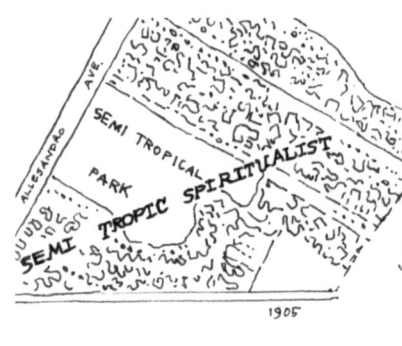

In 1905, the Semi~Tropic Spiritualist Association purchased a tract of land outside the city limits of Los Angeles. At this site, a community formed around a shared search for knowledge extending beyond the conscious mind.

Very few traces of the original Semi~Tropic park remain today. Although we may not be able to return to the physical location where the Semi~Tropic Spiritualists once walked, we can still follow in their paths.

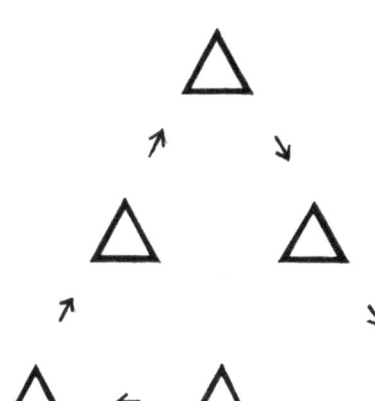

Please use this booklet, and the questions it contains, to guide your journey through the Semi~Tropic Spiritualist Pilgrimage Site.

Mark your time spent at each location with the stamp provided.

Begin your pilgrimage here

Palm Tree
History / Legacy

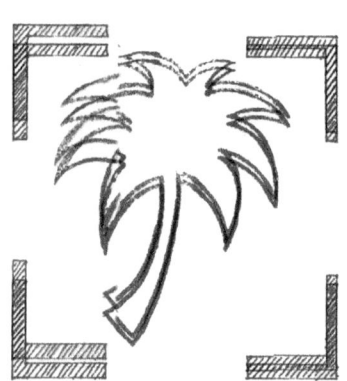

→ What was the first question?
→→ What were they looking for?
→→→ What can I learn from the searchers who went before me?

Hammer

Labor Foundation

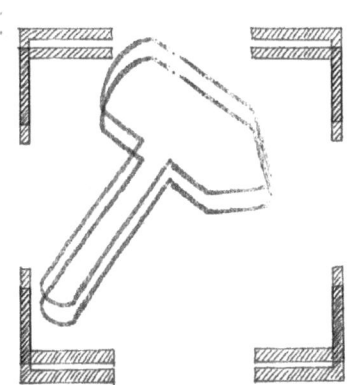

⇒ What is the first action I must take?
⇒ How do I genuinely commit?
⇒ How can I build something of meaning today?

Tent

Camp Community

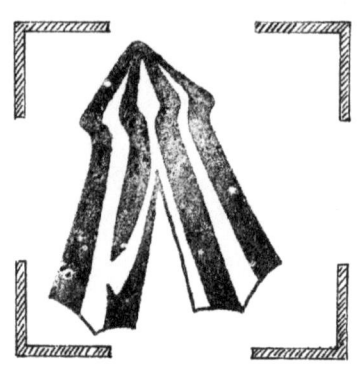

→ How do I move beyond myself?
→ How do I locate my community?
→ What can we accomplish together?

Candle

Knowledge
Learning

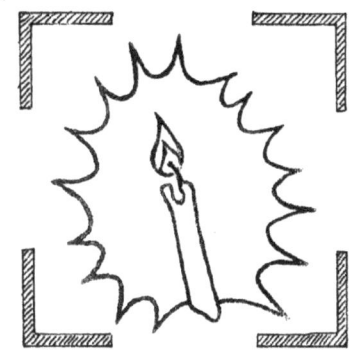

→ What guides our search?
→ How do we live in an enlightened way?
→ What do we do when the answers are not enough?

Pendulum

Mystery Divination

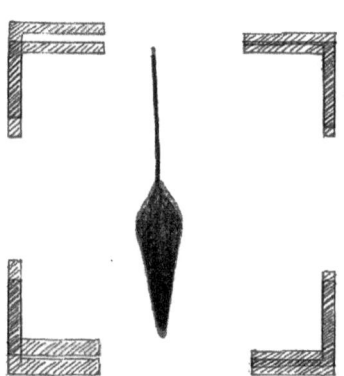

→ What is the space beyond our knowledge?
→ How do we avoid becoming lost in the darkness?
→ Where will the unknown take us?

Triple Pyramid
Exploration
Ascension

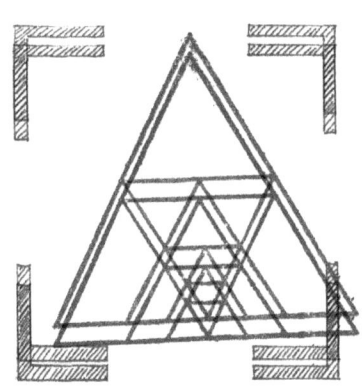

⇒ Why do we desire the next question?
⇒ How do we find the next question?
⇒ What is the next question?

Thank you for visiting the Semi~Tropic Spiritualist Pilgrimage Site. The relics you have seen are physical reminders of where we have come from, and pose questions regarding where we go next.

As you complete your journey here today, take the answers that you have found as you move forward on your path.

Ever there floats before the real
the bright, the beautiful ideal.

from Andrew Jackson Davis, The Children's Progressive Lyceum: A Manual (1867)

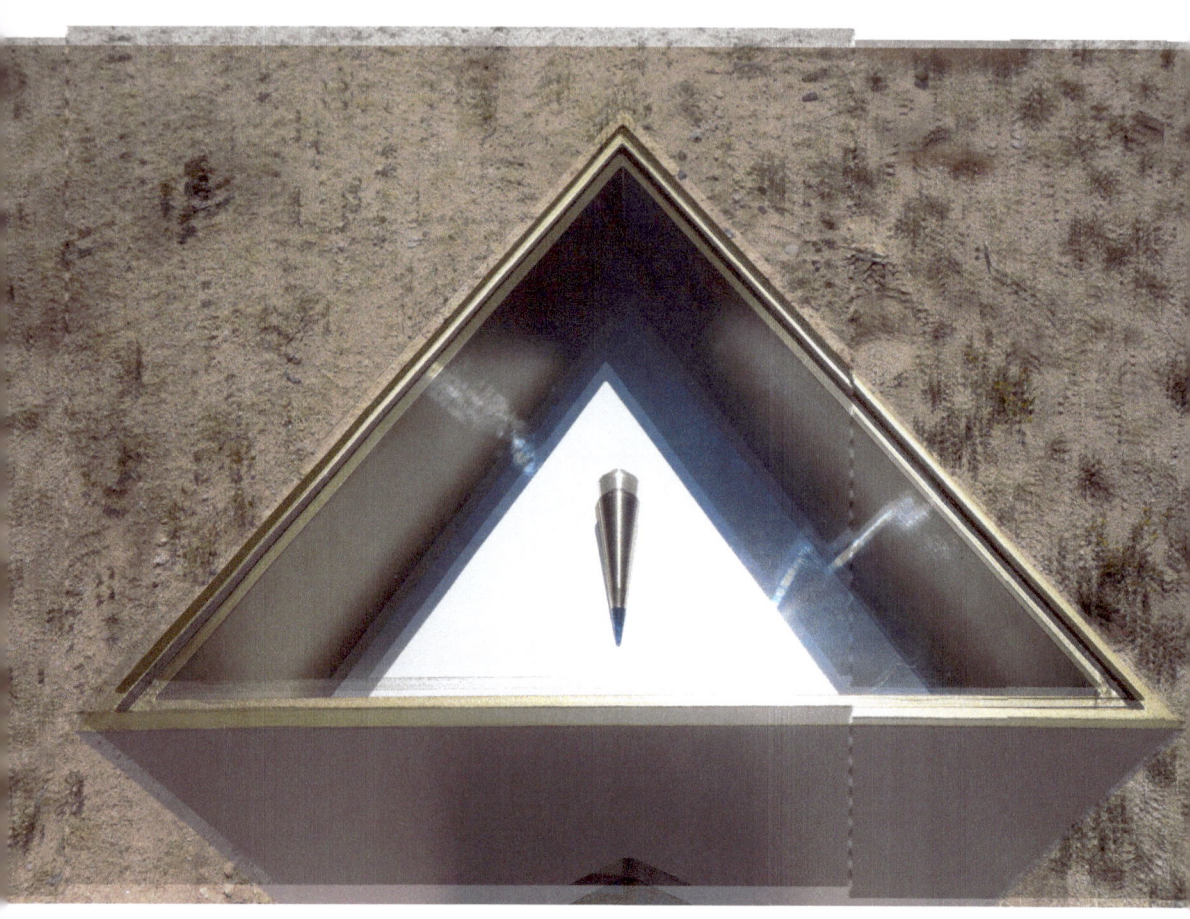

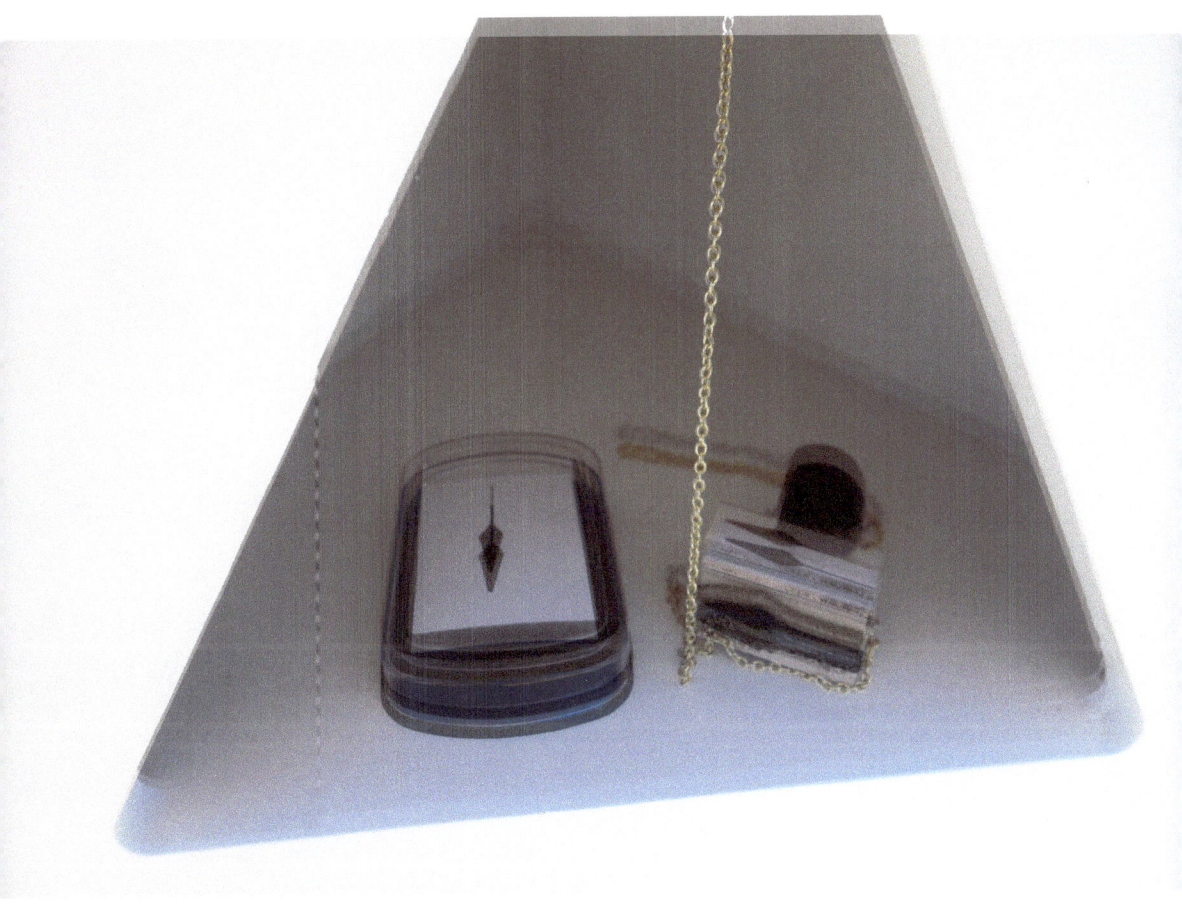

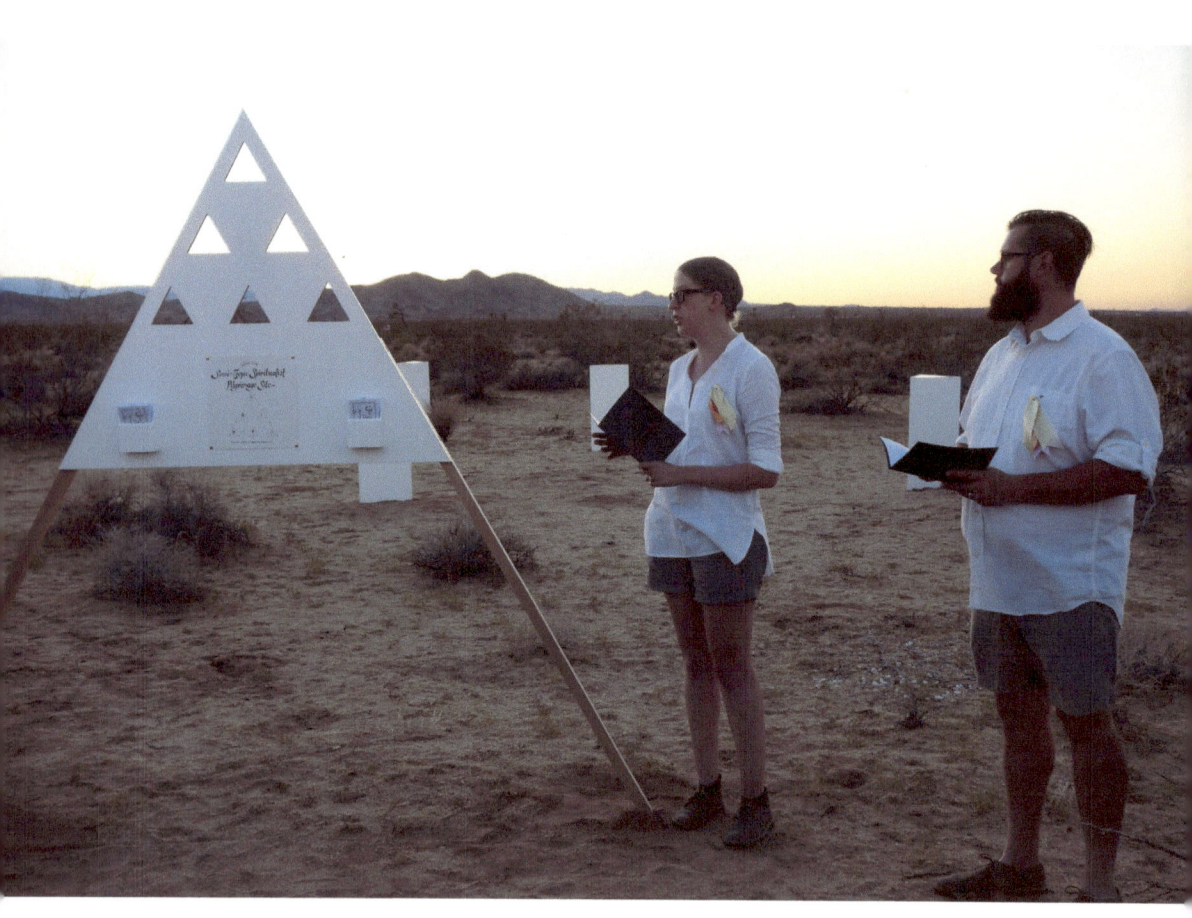

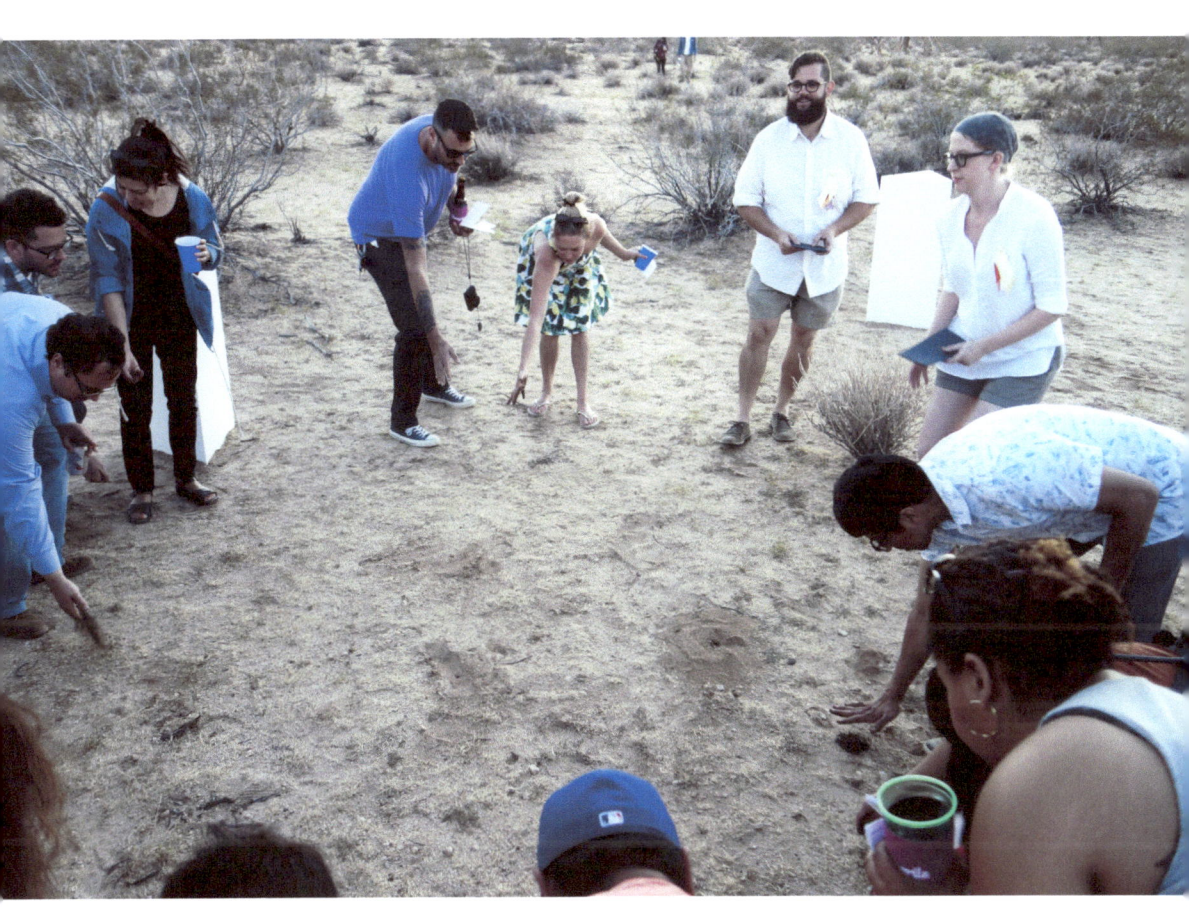

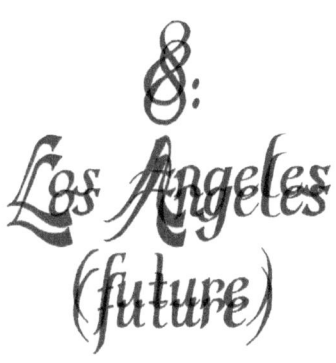

Semi-Tropic Spiritualist Test Site No. 7

As the Semi-Tropic Spiritualists, we have spent significant time thinking about where we have come from. We have examined the geographies of past utopian efforts and we have created new encampments. We have questioned our motivations and intentions and we have built the fire of our own community and values. For this Test Site, we returned home to Los Angeles. Following the example of our predecessors, we once again built a gathering point on a hillside overlooking the city, and presented our motivations, goals, and services to all who came to visit.

Now, as we move into the future, the Semi-Tropic Spiritualists invite you to join us in our path forward.

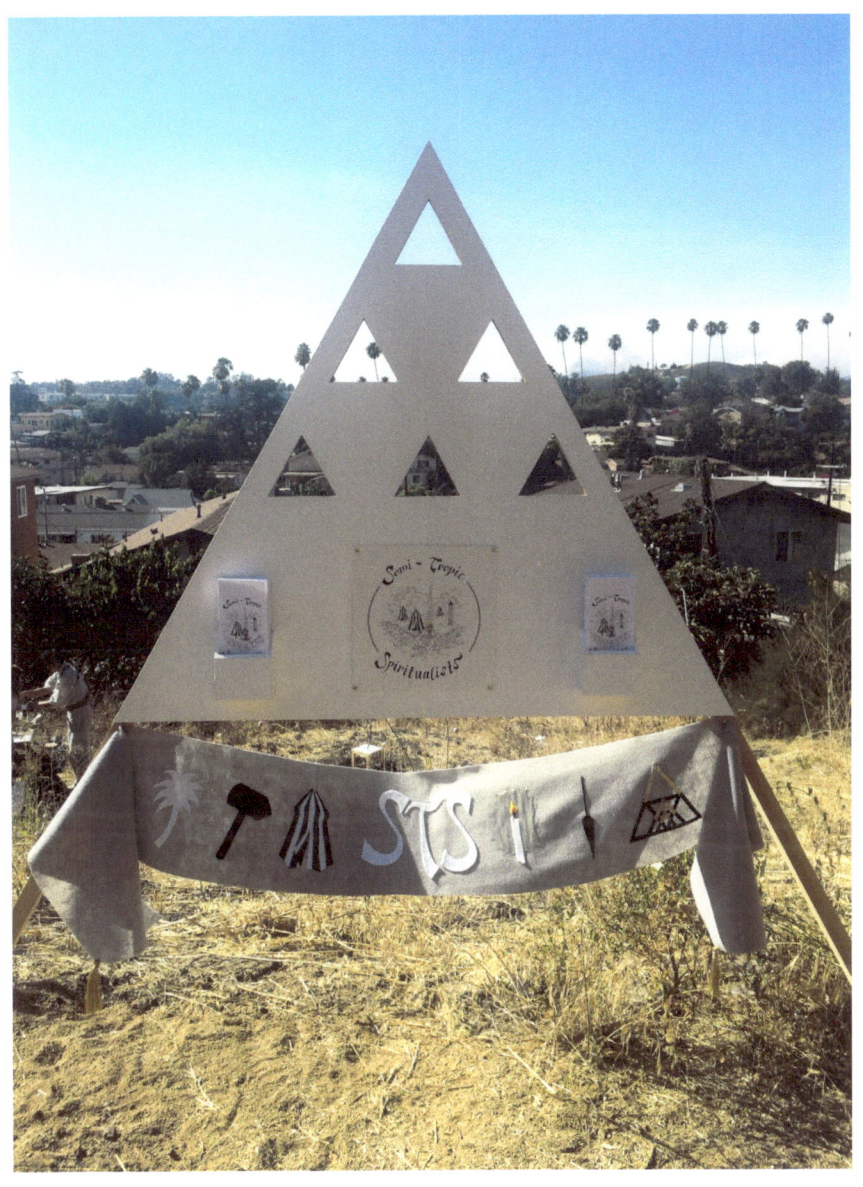

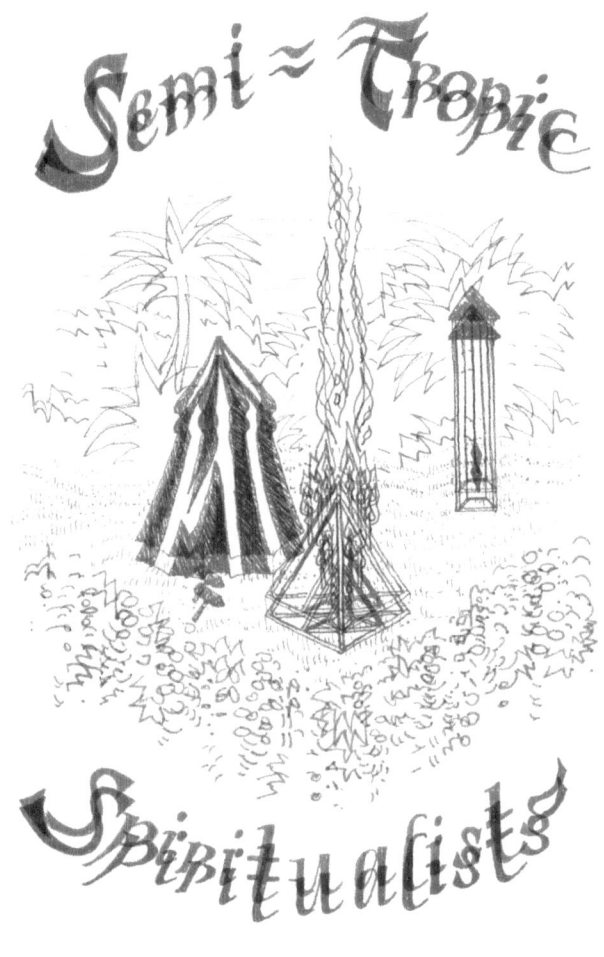

Semi-Tropic Spiritualists

Your Questions Answered

Who are the Semi~Tropic Spiritualists?

In 1905, the Semi~Tropic Spiritualist Association purchased a tract of land outside the city limits of Los Angeles. At this site a campsite community was formed around a shared search for knowledge extending beyond the conscious mind.

Today, the Semi~Tropic Spiritualists are once again active in Los Angeles and beyond. They have traveled from the majestic deserts of Joshua Tree, to the ruins of Llano del Rio, to the mountain valley of The Hatchery in Badger, CA, sharing their quest for knowledge through the **Path of Questioning** with hundreds of listeners.

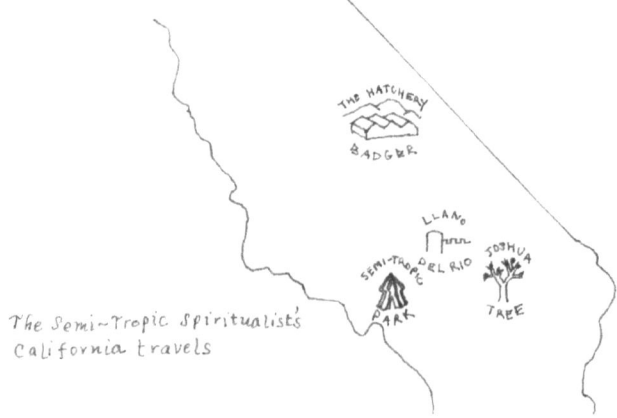

The Semi~Tropic Spiritualists California travels

What are the Semi-Tropic Spiritualists' Values and Goals?

The Semi-Tropic Spiritualists of today share with their predecessors a desire for knowledge beyond the conscious mind. They believe that this knowledge can only be reached through a community of seekers, coming together to follow a path of continuous exploration, guided by a philosophy of questioning. **Our knowledge ascends through this life and beyond.**

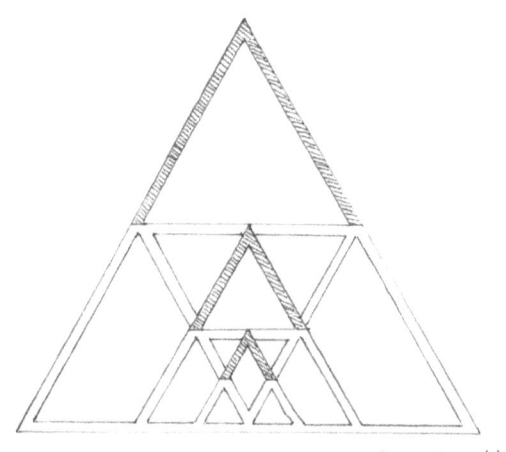

The Triple Pyramid of Ascention and Exploration

What can the Semi-Tropic Spiritualists Do For You?

The Semi-Tropic Spiritualists are available to present interactive lectures, displays, rituals and tests — all with the goal of helping you live in a more enlightened way. Through the use of divination tools, including:

- ▲ Pendulums
- ▲ Bells
- ▲ Symbology Cards
- ▲ Divination Tables
- ▲ Divination Boards
- ▲ Planchettes

and more, the Semi-Tropic Spiritualists want to help you access answers to your own deepest questions. Their Path of Questioning and Semi-Tropic Spiritualist's Symbol System will assist you in uncovering truths and revealing the unknown.

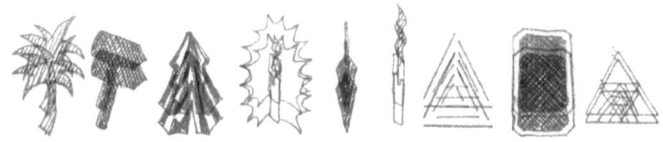

How can you join the Semi-Tropic Spiritualists?

The Semi-Tropic Spiritualists originally formed as a community—and while their physical campsite may no longer be present, they invite you to join them as they re-form their camp and

We Build Our Fire Where We Stand.

For more information, please fill out the form below and mail it, along with a self-addressed, stamped envelope to:

Semi-Tropic Spiritualists
3925 Division Street
Los Angeles, CA 90065

☐ YES, SEND ME MORE INFORMATION ABOUT THE SEMI-TROPIC SPIRITUALISTS

☐ YES, I AM INTERESTED IN JOINING THE SEMI-TROPIC SPIRITUALISTS

NAME _____

ADDRESS _____

CITY _____ STATE _____ ZIP _____

EMAIL _____

WHAT AM I SEARCHING FOR? _____

Conclusion: Semi-Tropic Park (interior)

In creating works as the Semi-Tropic Spiritualists, we have thought extensively about the dynamics of belief and the communities that arise from a desire to manifest conceptual ideals in real-world contexts. We have asked ourselves what it means to translate metaphysical concepts into physical form. We have created our own symbols, rituals, objects and spaces as a way to examine the goals and legacies of communities built around shared beliefs and a desire for a transformed reality. We have traveled around California, attempting to learn from the spaces once inhabited by the seekers and visionaries who came before us.

Now, after we have mapped our journeys and contemplated our paths, we find ourselves being drawn inward, away from the geographies previously traveled, moving the locus of our investigation toward internal experience. Rather than ask where the Semi-Tropic Spiritualists can re-build their fire or re-establish a camp, we are considering the desire for personal, practical efficacy that often accompanies the development of metaphysical or spiritual practices. As we travel inward and continue to create new Test Sites, we want to consider the question—what can the Semi-Tropic Spiritualists do for you?

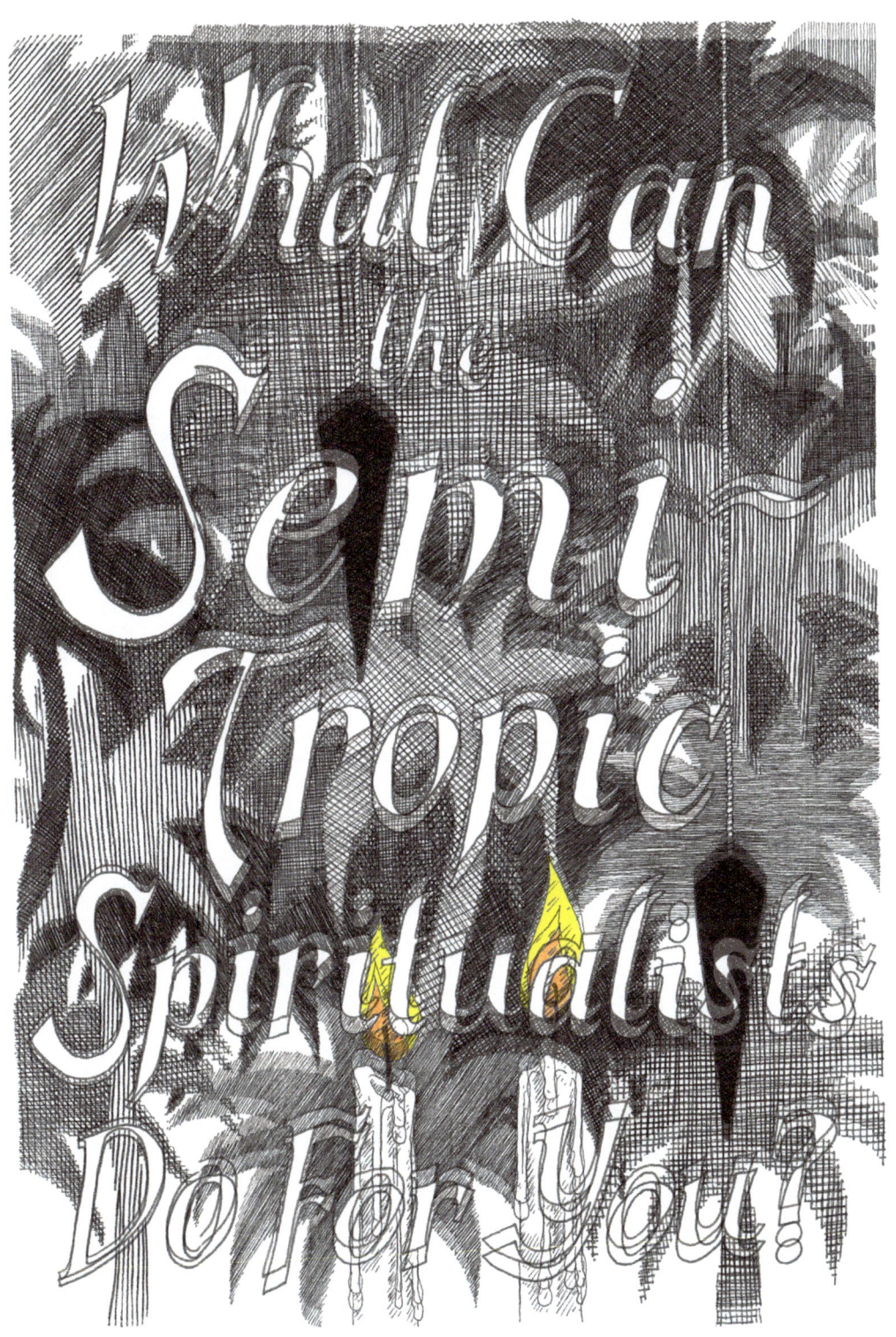

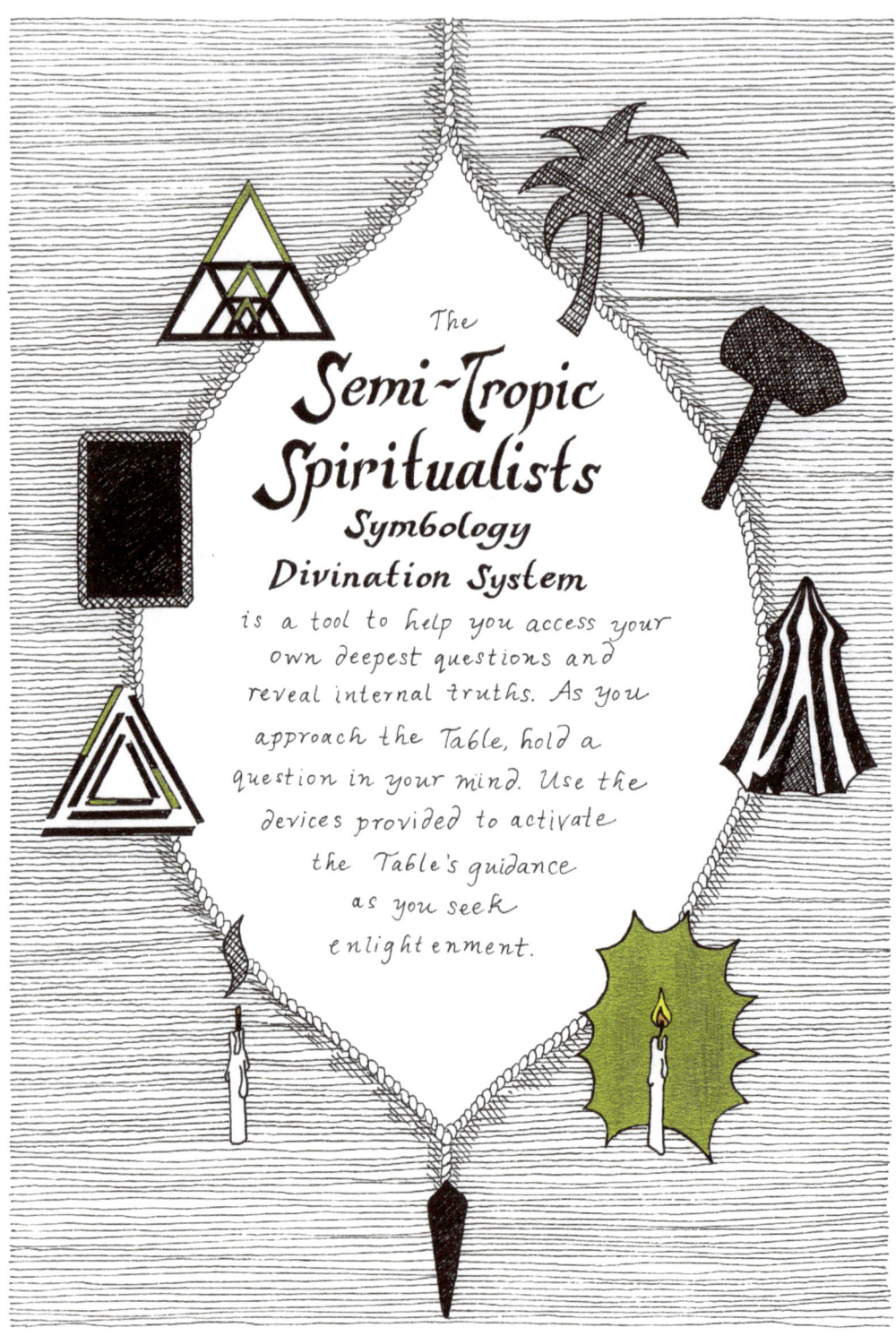

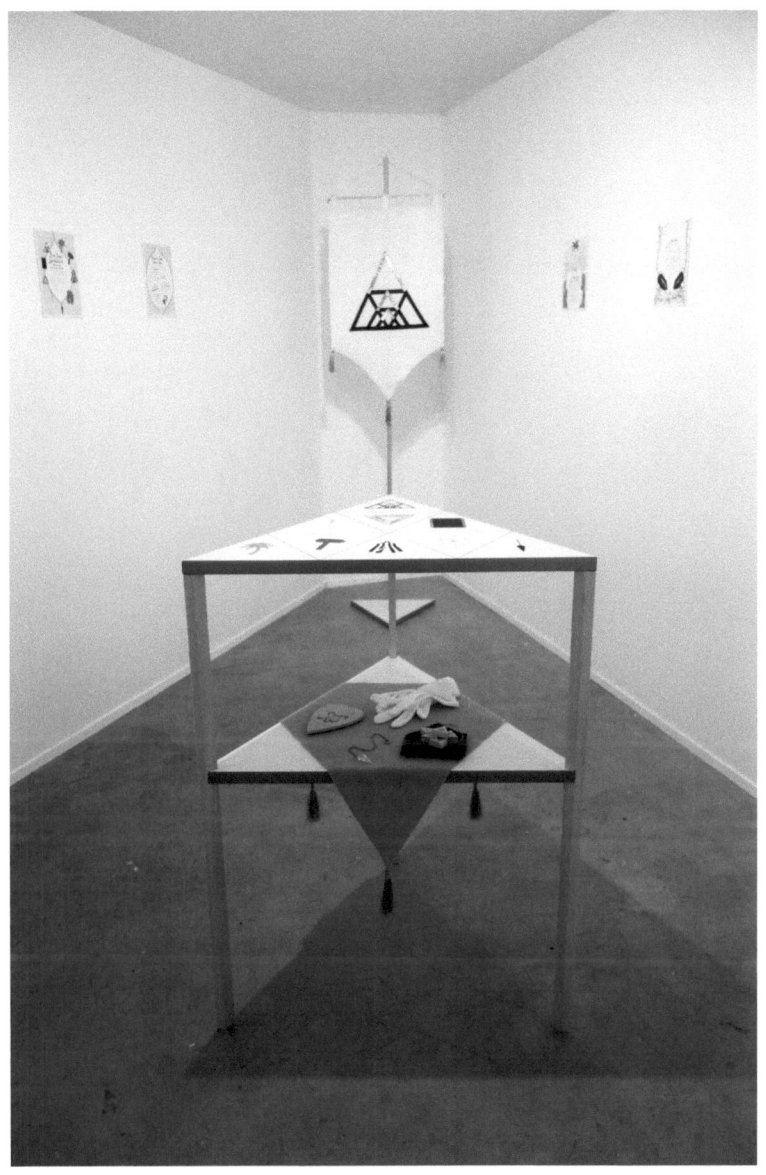

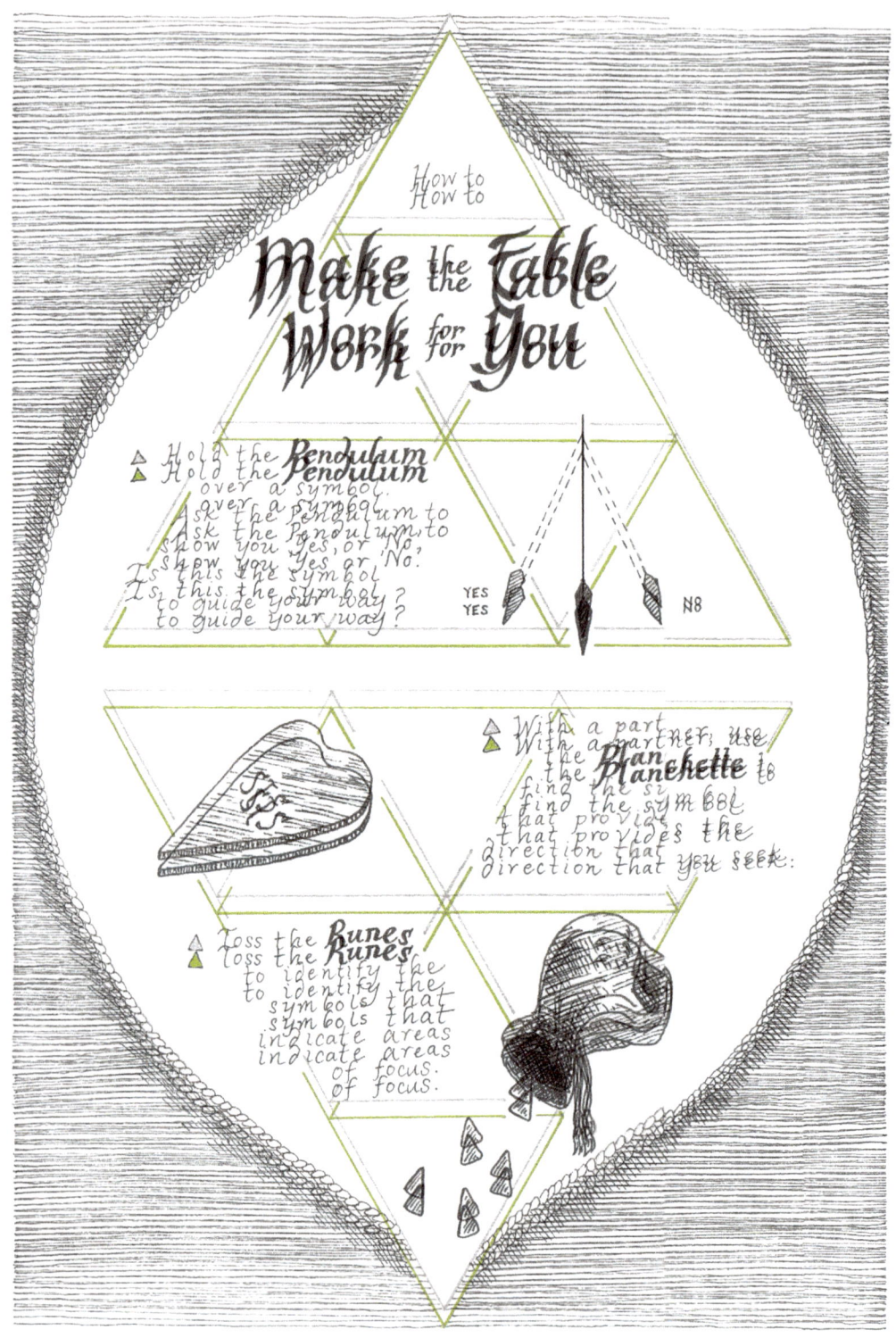

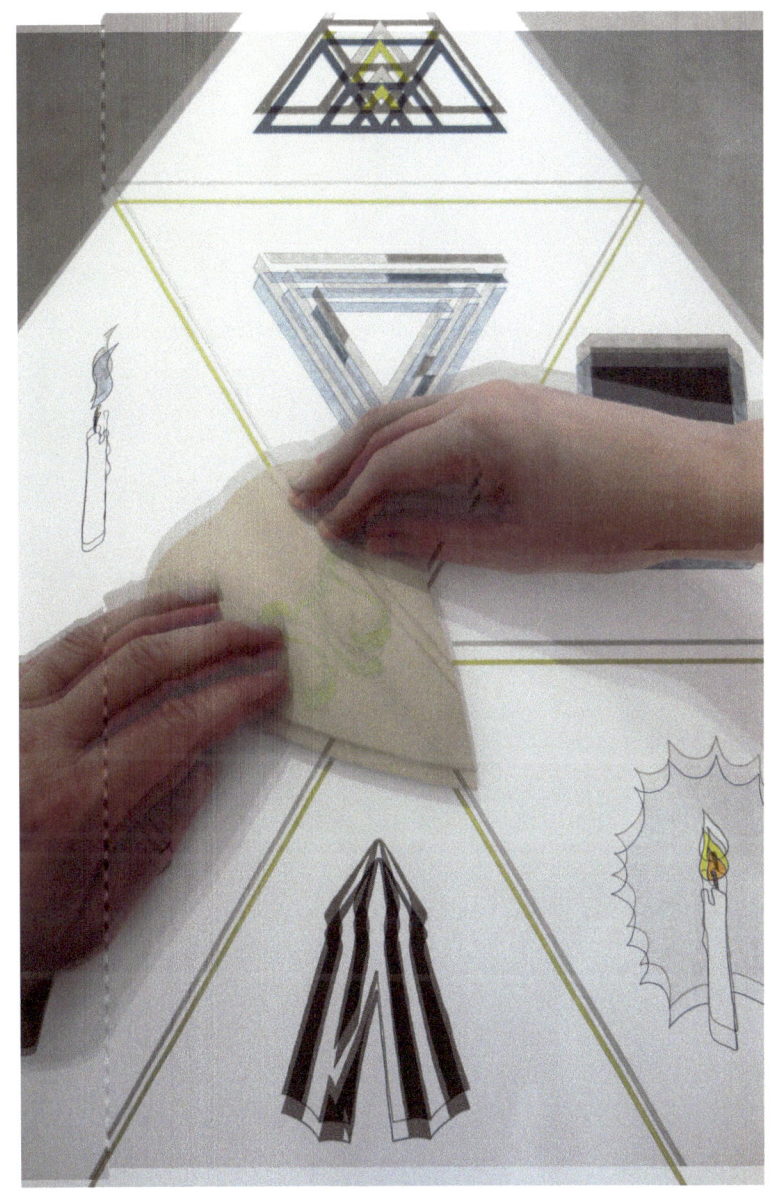

Semi-Tropic Spiritualists Exhibition Record

Test Site No. 1
LA Road Concerts: Mulholland Dérive, Los Angeles, CA, 2012

Test Site No. 2
Sanctified: Spirituality in Contemporary Art, Vincent Price Art Museum, Monterey Park, CA, 2013
Turbulent Times: First It's the Afterparty, Chime and Co., Los Angeles, CA, 2013
Unconfirmed Makeshift Museum, Klowden Mann, Los Angeles, CA, 2017

Test Site No. 3
Shangrila: Burrito Deluxe, Shangrila, Joshua Tree, CA, 2013
Squaring the Circle, Llano del Rio, CA, 2014

Test Site No. 4
Haunted, Cultural Alliance of Long Beach, Long Beach, CA, 2013
The White Album, Richard Telles Fine Art, Los Angeles, CA, 2014

Test Site No. 5
God Will Not Have His Work Made Manifest By Cowards, The Hatchery, Badger, CA, 2014

Test Site No. 6
Peak Experiences, Shangrila, Joshua Tree, 2015
What Can the Semi-Tropic Spiritualists Do For You?, General Projects, Los Angeles, CA, 2018

Test Site No. 7
Unseen, Summercamp Project Project, Los Angeles, CA, 2016

Test Site No. 8
Untested Address, Unconfirmed Makeshift Museum, Irvine, CA, 2017

Test Site No. 9
What Can the Semi-Tropic Spiritualists Do For You?, General Projects, Los Angeles, CA, 2018

Photo Credits

The majority of the imagery contained in this edition is from The Semi-Tropic Spiritualists, Astri Swendsrud & Quinn Gomez Heitzeberg.

The following images are used with permission from the photographers:

Cover image: Joel Woodman

Pages 10, 11 & 23: Diana-Sofia Estrada

Pages 15, 30 & 31: Jim Heizeberg

Page 44: Bianca D'Amico

Page 45: Joel Woodman

Pages 65-73: Anthony Bodlović & Ronald Dzerigian

Pages 104, 105: Christina Ondrus

www.ingramcontent.com/pod-product-compliance
Lightning Source LLC
Chambersburg PA
CBHW051945210526
45473CB00006B/2395